A Liverpool Streetwise Kid

THE EARLY YEARS

Charlie Seiga

First published 2005

This edition published by
The Picture Book Corporation Ltd. 2005

www.picture-book.co.uk

e-mail: info@picture-book.co.uk

ISBN 1-84651-001-5

I would like to dedicate this book to my late mother, my sister Delia and my brothers Jimmy, Ged and Freddy. I don't know if I was ever worthy of their unshakable loyalty and love, but they were people who I would have willingly died for.

I would also like to thank all those friends of mine, who are good people with decency and honour, for all the continued loyalty and support they gave me while I was going through hard times. There are too many names to mention but you know that I know who you all are.

Charlie Seiga

FOREWORD

I have often been asked by the readers of my other books, as well as friends and family over the years, why I didn't write more about my childhood days in Killer, the international best selling book I penned during my time on trial for murder. Well I do talk about my childhood in that book, but only a brief page or two. They always wanted to know more about my family, my school days, what I got up to as a streetwise kid in the 1940's and 1950's and how I became a villain. So I decided to complete my autobiographical trilogy with the story of my childhood years just for them. I hope you enjoy reading this book as I journey back through both happy and sad times in my young life.

I would also like to take this opportunity to remind you of how harsh times were then, when people went hungry and food was rationed. There was no way out for some people, but I found my own way out, as I lived on the streets and survived on the streets. As they say 'if you can control the streets you can control the people' and I was the type of kid who if stranded in the desert would somehow find a glass of water.

I always tell the truth and nothing but the truth so help me god, well to a certain extent that is. After all, we all tell little white lies now and again, don't we?

"We know you fuckin' killed him. We have got you bang to rights this time Charlie. There's no way you are going to walk on this, not this time!" These were the hushed words of the detective who was standing behind me. I was sat at a table in a police interview room accompanied by two snide looking detectives. The one behind me had leaned over to me close and whispered into my ear so the tape couldn't pick him up. This was even before I had been cautioned and while I was still being interviewed, accused of pumping three bullets into another villain's head.

How many times have I heard those words before (we've got you bang to rights) in past interviews and past charges over the years?

Liverpool, June 2002

Here I am just chilling out, sitting here a free man once again relaxing at the side of the swimming pool, soaking up the sun in the privacy of my own beautiful garden. I live in a fairly large detached house in a quiet residential area of suburban Liverpool. However, life wasn't always this sweet for me. In the early years my life was hard ~ very hard – there was no way I was ever born with a silver spoon in my mouth ~ I had to get out, get off my arse and I did what I had to do in order to achieve this wonderful life I now enjoy.

I think I will start my story here just before I go back in time, back to when I was just a kid living in poverty and running the streets:~ it is a beautiful, hot summers afternoon and it is so peaceful just lying here the smell of freshly cut lawns and scent of summertime flowers are everywhere, even the wild garden birds seem to be singing their heads off just for me; what more could a man want? To be honest though, I am actually recuperating after last night's hectic events. I had a party at my house and it was a bit of a mad one! It must have only ended at about ten o'clock this morning and I am now suffering really badly. I have got the shakes and feel dead sick in my stomach. I've also got a really bad hangover, which is typical of me when I have been out clubbing it and partying. 'Never again!' How many times have we all said those words after a night out getting bladderd?

My two mates, Mark, Jimmy and me were clubbing it in town last night and like everything else that happens with our crowd, one thing leads to another. Nearly everyone goes out and 'cops off' at the weekends in Liverpool. The nightlife is 'boss'.

I mostly hang around the Mosquito Club, Metro and News Bars along with the Living Room on Victoria Street. As well as those there are lots more good clubs and bars to choose from but these are my favourites. This is where it is all happening now and you often see a lot of celebrities in Liverpool enjoying the nightlife and buzz in that locality. Yeah — thinking back, last night was some night! Some of the carryings on were crazy. But right this minute I am chilling out good style. We had met four cracking girls in one of the clubs last night and I can honestly say they were all good-looking, beautiful, young women ~ like the majority of young scouse birds are. We all decided to go back to my house. Now this is about four o'clock in the morning and it is practically getting light outside, the sun was just starting to rise and you could even hear the milkman clanking his bottles down the road. We had all had a good laugh with these girls last night so they came back with us – nothing funny in it, they were just your mad type of party girls. It then comes out that they work in one of the top lap dancing bars in the city; it was Angels I found out later. Now I've got nothing against lap dancing bars or lap dancers for that matter, after all they are only young girls trying to earn a few quid. It doesn't necessarily mean that they are sleazy or anything. Most probably the old 'perves' that go in there watching them are though. But yeah – good luck to them if they can get a few quid out of them.

We had only been in the house five minutes and the girls had completely stripped off 'bollock'o' and are running around the pool screaming and trying to push each other in. That's what most scouse birds are like – just out for a laugh and a buzz, and these girls were definitely that! In fact, most Liverpool people are like that – its what I could only describe as a unique sense of humour that we have all got! Everybody likes to take the piss out of each other but its harmless fun and not meant offensively, the majority of us are just out for a laugh. And the girls were no exception.

At one point, one of the girls was about to get off in a local taxi, which had pulled up outside my house. She gets into the taxi and her mate was leaning over the cab window saying her goodbyes – the way birds do – but she had absolutely nothing on now except her thong! Bearing in mind it is now broad daylight and about eight o'clock in the morning, I shouted to her from my front door which was wide open, "Hey, do us a favour love and cover yourself up or put a towel round you". I mean, I live in a fairly quiet suburban area and one of my neighbours was already out mowing his front lawn.

The poor man nearly had a heart attack when he saw this model like lap dancer with nothing on but a thong. She turned around laughing when I said this, then she cheekily slapped her own arse and shouted to me "Chill out Charlie' just turn the sounds up will yer! I'll only be a minute!" What could I do? Trust me to end up with a mad lap dancer!

I am sixty-two and have finally reached a crossroad in my life, or at least I think I have. Who would have thought I would have ended up this way? Is this what I have been surviving all my life for? Was it worth it, did it pay for me? Have I really achieved everything I ever wanted? I don't think so – 'cos although I have now passed sixty my mind is still young and active. I still have some friends who are the same age as me but they seem to have aged considerably. And yet, I don't really mean physically, but in a mental sense. Their outlook on life is sad; I don't mean this in a nasty way but in the sense that they are disappointed and seem to have a bitter outlook. It is like they have given up on life and I can't socialise with people like that. Now don't get me wrong, we all go on a downer from time to time and feel pessimistic. But these people are constantly like that! I mean, I still have plenty of dreams and I am still very ambitious. I have got plenty of go left in me. I have always been a dreamer and have had aspirations all my life, in fact I believe that without your dreams you are nothing, but that's only my opinion.

Throughout my life I have always felt as if I am going to die tomorrow and that maybe I am running out of time. It is 'cos I feel that way that I still have this burning desire to grab what I can and enjoy life to the full while it lasts.

In the past, I have been classed as a ruthless villain or as a gangster. Well that is what the Liverpool police and the newspapers had me down as! I have always denied ever being a gangster~ but everywhere I went, my friends and I always maintained certain principles. We would never harm the ordinary man, woman or child in the street, like the scum of today who have no respect do. There was always a certain line to be drawn and a very strict code of conduct that we all lived by. In the past I have been charged with some very serious offences indeed. Somehow though, I wasn't convicted for most of these crimes. I remember somebody wrote about me being the 'Houdini of the criminal world' – another newspaper called me the 'Teflon Don' – nothing ever stuck to me! All this speculation and what the press has written is a load of rubbish as far as I am concerned. Maybe I was born with one of the greatest gifts a person could ever possess – luck! I was born on the seventh day, the seventh child, and with seven brothers and they say that seven is a lucky number – well it certainly has been for me. Lets face it, at my age and the way I have been living it must be.

Now I am not a superstitious person or anything like that but when I was an eleven-year-old kid, a gypsy woman once told me that I would always have luck for the rest of my life. Sometimes, I keep reminiscing about the past, and occasionally the gypsy woman. I keep thinking about how it all started, so long ago in another place and another time….

Huyton, Liverpool 1951

"I want you to swear and promise me, not to tell anyone Charlie!" she said, "I swear to God! I wont tell anybody!" I replied. "That's a good boy, now off you go home before it gets too dark - tomorrow is the big day!" the gypsy woman said. It was a bitter cold winter's afternoon and now nighttime was fast approaching. It was almost four o'clock - that's when all the kids are coming home from school. Not me though! As usual, I had been sagging school (playing truant). I got up off the old polished wooden box I always sat on when I was in her caravan - it was next to the roaring fire glowing in the cast iron stove. On top of the old stove was a big metal chimney pipe that went right up and out through a hole in the roof of the caravan. It was always hot, and many a time I had almost burnt my finger tips on it. When I got to the door of the caravan, I didn't really want to leave, as it was so warm and snug in there. Rowena (that was the gypsy woman's name) gave me a loving hug and smiled warmly. She resembled my own mother in a funny sort of way; she had flowing long dark hair and dark brown eyes, yet her smile was just something else, all warm and friendly. But then there were times when she could be so serious, like when she told me tales abut her travels - countries she had been to, things she had seen, it was so exciting and it fascinated me. I was completely spellbound by her.

There was also a very sad side to her. She once told me she had had a son who when he was just seventeen joined the army back in 1940 - coincidentally, that was the year that I was born. The Second World War was raging then and her only son was killed somewhere fighting in France. I hated to see her so sad when she spoke of her dead son. She would always cling to me at those moments and tell me, "No harm will ever come to you Charlie because you are so lucky. You have that special gift and nobody will ever take it away from you!"

I can remember vividly the day I first met Rowena - I was sagging school again. To be honest, I never really went to school. I always bunked off and went on my 'adventures', sometimes taking some of my mates with me, but mostly I would bunk off alone. I would sooner be off in the vast open fields and course woodland on the city outskirts, than stuck in some stuffy classroom, bored to death - I just didn't like school, it wasn't for me. It was 1951, I had just turned 11 years of age and I was on one of my 'adventures' in a place called Knowsley a small village surrounded by farms, woodlands and meadows, just five miles or so from Liverpool itself. On the edge of one of these Knowsley meadows was where I first set eyes on the gypsy camp. It was a spectacular site to see, all this through the eyes of an eleven-year-old kid. I was totally in awe of it all. The caravans were all horse drawn and of different shapes and sizes. Some had been painted yellow and red with green canvas roofs. The horses and ponies that pulled them were magnificent! It reminded me of when I used to go to the pictures (cinemas as they are now called) to see a good 'Cowboy and Indian' film with my mates. The gypsy camp just looked like the Red Indians and Cowboy camps that we saw on the big screen. Funnily enough I always stuck up for the Indians when I was a kid, I don't now why, 'cos they were always portrayed as the 'baddies'. Cowboy pictures were all the rage with kids having heroes like Roy Rodgers, Gene Autry and Hop Along Cassidy ~ but they weren't mine. I always stuck up for the baddies. I can't explain this, but I did. When the baddies came on screen everybody in the picture house would 'boo' and when the goodies came on everyone shouted 'hooray', well everyone except me that is! Anyway after seeing all this excitement ahead of me I sort of cheekily, or come to think about it - quite boldly, walk over to one of the ponies that was tethered to a tree by the side of one the nicest looking caravans I had ever seen in my life. I cautiously started to stroke the pony, after a minute or so, I heard the caravan creak and it moved slightly. When I looked up this gypsy woman was staring at me. I had the strangest feeling that she knew me the way she just kept looking at me. I didn't feel scared of her or anything, but strangely enough I felt as if I knew her too. I just never could explain why it seemed that way. "What's your name then?" she said in a soft, gentle voice. I told her my name and she beckoned me over to her by the caravan steps, I sort of slowly sauntered over to her. "You are not from around these parts are you'?" she asked - I just shook my head. "Come on now, tell me what you have been up to then and why aren't you in school". I shrugged my shoulders and stood there not really knowing what to say. "Have you eaten? You look cold and hungry to me, come on inside and get yourself warm, I'll get you something to eat." she said enticingly.

Poverty was still rife in Liverpool even though the war had been over for four to five years by now. People were still finding it very hard to survive, especially the kids. I though was becoming a streetwise survivor ~ living on my wits. I had already eaten that morning on my way through the village. I had taken a bottle of milk from the milk cart that was parked outside some cottages, and I had also swiped a nougat bar and a packet of wine gums from the local sweet shop, but I couldn't tell her that now, could I?

Well, that was the introduction and beginning of my relationship with Rowena, the gypsy woman.

"Hurry home before it gets too dark Charlie and remember to be up bright and early tomorrow!" With her words still ringing in my ears I jogged along the narrow country lane, which led away from the gypsy camp. It was getting quite dark now and the shadows were drawing in but I wasn't scared, in fact I felt quite the opposite. I felt myself getting all excited again thinking what tomorrow would bring. I began to run faster and faster towards my home, which was in Huyton, Liverpool 14. I was starting to panic a little knowing full well that if I arrived home late I would be sent to bed with no tea. Or worse still, get a good hiding if my Mam or Dad found out I had been bunking off school. On second thoughts, I told myself, why should I worry, I won't be living there after tomorrow, I am going away with Rowena, she is taking me with her. All the rest of the gypsies are breaking camp in the morning and I am going to be with them forever and ever. I still have to keep my sworn secret though, and not to tell anybody at home about it all. I had promised Rowena. I will do anything for her ~ I love her, not in a dirty way but in a nice warm and affectionate way. I loved the way we always sat by her fire in her caravan and she told me the stories of long ago. She told me that the caravans that all the gypsies have now are the latest models – and are barrel shaped. They had to be because the older types had the wheels on the outside of the caravan, and that wasn't good because the bad men who drove big motor wagons on the highways, used to deliberately bump into the wooden wheels of the caravans and break them. That would put the gypsies off the road for hours. Well at least until they could repair their wheels again. It was an early form of the road rage that goes on today!

The lorry drivers also blamed the gypsy caravans for being too slow on the roadways, especially if they were driving behind them and wanted to get to their destinations more quickly with their deliveries. But now that the gypsies had made the latest barrel designs their wheels were tucked further underneath, and of course this prevented the big lorries from breaking them. Everything was done for a reason. She told me that the way the caravan was designed, even down to the beautiful wood carvings that decorated the outside of the caravan, including the wheels and the pony shafts was purely functional. A lot of the wood was carved away, not just to make it ornate looking, but to make the caravan lighter in weight and that would ease the burden for the pony to pull, especially on long journeys over the countryside. Another fascinating fact about the design work was that if the weather was really rough the carved design prevented the gale force winds from blowing it over - even in open fields - simply because the wind would blow though the wooden wheels and over and around the barrel shaped roof.

Everything Rowena told me was truly amazing. She even taught me lots of things I would never otherwise have known about. Who needs school? Not me, and hopefully I wont be attending them ever again. After being in deep thought while still running along I realised I was not too far away from my home - maybe a mile or so away at the most. I had finally reached the main road now and I could see all the lights on in the shops and houses where I live in Huyton. I know I'm late, and I'm dreading what awaits me when I finally arrive at our house.

"What time is this?" my mother said as I walked through the front door of our house. Incidentally most people left the front door of their houses open or ajar in those days. Neighbours trusted each other and people were cheery and carefree in an innocent sort of way. Not like it is nowadays, when people are being mugged and their homes being plundered by the scum of today. "Where have you been till this late? The other three had to come home on their own!" she said. It was nearly 5 o'clock and she was of course referring to my three younger brothers. It was always my responsibility to bring them home from school, and it was down to me to look after them with me being the oldest. "I had to stay behind in school Ma, the teacher made me write out two hundred lines as a punishment for talking in class." I replied. Discipline was very strict at our school; kids had to obey the rules. If you didn't God help you! Especially if you were given the cane, which I got on many occasions. "Hold out your hands Seiga." How many times have I heard those dreaded words from a teacher? That cane could leave your hands in agony for hours. Even more so if it connected with the soft flesh of your fingertips on a cold winter morning. But right here and now I am trying to convince my mother why I am late home from school, and not making a very good job of it. I knew I couldn't fool my Ma, she knew me like the back of her hand. Her dark eyes burning into me, as though she could read my innermost thoughts. I felt a hand grabbing the scruff of my neck - it was my old feller.

I was dreading facing him, he could be a real wicked bastard at times. "I know where you've been," he said, "you've been sagging school again haven't you?" I tried my best to deny it. "Don't tell me lies; the School Board man has been here today. You haven't been going to school - what have you been up to eh? You lying little sod!" he shouted. I knew what was coming next. He started laying into me with his leather belt - I could feel it on my legs and arms as I crouched down on the floor. My old feller was far too heavy handed. I hated him – I always did. Not just because of the beating he was giving me now, but he was and always has been a selfish man. He treated my mother like a dog at times, and when he was out he was always in the alehouse, returning home pissed most nights of the week. He had a violent temper when he kicked off, which I was getting the brunt of right now.

"That's enough!" I heard my mother shout, "leave him alone; I will chastise him myself." My mother had now positioned herself between me and my dad, attempting to protect me and telling him to lay off. "You're going too far!" she said.

"You're always the same," he said to her "just because he is your blue eye" it was true what he said, my mother did have a soft spot for me, I was her favourite, and I knew it. She had always spoilt me over the years. "Get up those stairs," he shouted at me "you're going to bed with no tea." Just as I was about to climb the stairs he gave me a kick, the hard metal toecap of his boot caught me square on the top of my leg. I winced in pain and crawled up the stairs to bed as fast as I could.

The bed that my brothers and I slept in was a big old-fashioned thing. It must have in made in the 1930's or 40's and was covered with some big, heavy, grey, woollen blankets and on top of them was thrown an old army overcoat. The overcoat was to keep us 'extra warm' my Ma used to say, particularly at winter times. It used to be absolutely freezing in the winter in those houses - there was no such thing as central heating or electric blankets at that time in the late 40's or 50's. I remember we would wake up on a bitter winter morning and the frost would be on the inside of the bedroom windows. My brothers and I used to play oxo, scratching off the noughts and crosses in the frost on the windowpanes with our little fingers.

After lying in bed shivering and licking my wounds I could hear my parents still arguing downstairs. Some time later it finally went quiet down stairs and after a while my three younger brothers were sent up to bed. My brother's names were Billy - he was eighteen months younger than me, then there was Jimmy, who was about two years younger than Billy, and finally, Joe who was considered the 'baby'. I think he was about 6 or 7 at the time. Nevertheless, when all four of us were in that big old bed we soon got snug and warm. Our Billy had sneaked me a 'jam buttie' up from the kitchen. I couldn't thank him enough as by that time I was starving and I quickly wolfed it down. My three younger brothers always looked up to me as their 'big brother' that could look after them and protect them, particularly from any bullies at school. I used to sort all that business out for them. They were very loyal to me, in as much as I could trust them to say fuck all about what I used to get up to, such as sagging school and a bit of pilfering here and there. They also loved me telling them stories; mainly about my little 'adventures', where I had been, what I had got up to, and so forth.

Most nights, when the four of us were tucked away in bed, I would get out my torch. It was a little flat one with an oval shaped light, which I used to have planted under a broken floorboard beneath our bed. We would all sit up with the clothes over us making a kind of tent shape. I would switch the torch on and begin telling them the stories. They were fascinated by it all! Mind you, I did have a vivid imagination and could exaggerate quite a bit - but that's kids for you! I remember one dark winter night we were all huddled up in our bed with our makeshift tent, my torch was glowing and I was telling them how I got saved from being killed that very day.

It all began, I told my brothers, when I was standing outside the famous Liver Buildings by the River Mersey. I was looking up at the buildings that were so high they seemed to practically touch the clouds. Suddenly, I heard this little squeaking and cheeping noise. I looked up again and near to the top of the building I could see there was a baby seagull trapped on one of the big windowsills. The poor thing seemed to be hanging down by its leg. I had better save it before it dies I thought, so I started to climb one of the big cast-iron drain pipes that lead up to where it was stranded.

While I was climbing I would occasionally glance down and I could see the people below were getting smaller and smaller - I must have been dead high up by now. I was also getting nervous and a bit scared, but I was determined to save that little bird. After climbing so high I finally reached the poor little thing. I clung to the drainpipe with one hand then I got hold of the little bird with my other hand releasing its tiny leg that was trapped. I managed to carefully put the frightened bird down my pullover - I could feel its tiny heart pounding with fright. I then started to slowly climb back down the drainpipe. I took another look down and there were now crowds of people looking up at me. Some were shouting for me to be careful and to take my time.

Just then I felt the drainpipe start to give and move away from the wall. I froze and stayed as still as I possibly could - now I was dead scared. I could hear the people below me screaming "Oh my God he's going to fall!" I tried to climb down once more, but it was too late. The pipe came away from the wall altogether, me with it. I started hurtling towards the ground, certain to be smashed to smithereens. Just then, from out of nowhere came two giant seagulls.

At this point in my story I paused under the blankets with my brothers and said "You must be getting tired I'll stop now, let's finish this another night!" Jimmy bounced up and down in eager anticipation "Aw Charlie, NO! You've got to finish it, what happened, what happened" he squealed excitedly. I grinned at them all as I had only been winding them up!

I resumed the story - my brothers' eyes were wide with excitement. I knew one of the seagulls, and it could talk to me – "Quickly Charlie grab our legs", it screeched. I reached out and grabbed their scaly legs. Then they softly glided with me back down to the ground and saved me. One of the giant seagulls tenderly took the little baby seagull from me in its beak and then they both flew away back into the clouds above. After I had finished my little yarn, our Billy being the oldest, and also being a bit sceptical for a kid, said, "I'm not having any of that. How come the seagulls knew you?" "Because I always feed them when I go to the pier head by the Mersey soft lad." I replied. Our Jimmy said "Aw Kid, that was a great story!" But now I was about to tell them a real story, about how I was going to run away in the morning with Rowena the gypsy woman. I knew my secret would be safe with them.

Billy and Jimmy idolised me and they would never say anything - that was for sure and our little Joe was too young to understand really. So here I am telling them all that I was going to run away tomorrow after I had taken them to School.

The next morning was yet another very cold winters day, my Mam always got us up from bed nice and early but she always had a roaring fire waiting for us. We could usually hear her clearing the grate out and raking the ashes before we got up and we were never allowed down stairs before it was good and ready. She always warmed our school clothes in front of that fire and we could sometimes see the damp coming off our jumpers before they were dry enough to wear. My Mam kept a regular routine She always made sure our appearance was good even though everyone was poor in those days. We were always reasonably dressed and well turned out. This was of course to ensure that we all had a good appearance in front of the schools teachers. There was nothing more embarrassing than a teacher pulling you out of a class to get a wash in the cloakroom, labelling you as a dirty little boy or girl. Discipline was always quite strict in our house with both of our parents always making sure we did as we were told. Before the four of us came back home from school we would inspect each other before going into the house and facing our ma. Checking each other carefully to ensure that our clothes were tidy and that our hands, faces, knees and particularly our shoes were clean. If they weren't clean enough we would be in big trouble. Every Saturday night was bath night for all four of us, and we would take it in turns one after the other to get into the scolding hot bath; even the brass taps on the bath were too hot to touch. She used to use carbolic soap to scrub us spotlessly clean and if you got that dreaded soap into your eyes it would sting for hours and hours. We couldn't complain though, as all we would get for our troubles was a smack across the back of our heads. Our ma was always worried about us catching things at school, especially nits. If she happened to catch one of us scratching our heads, "Come here" she would say. We would have to kneel down in front of her on the floor and put our heads in her lap ready for inspection with a fine toothcomb. All the while she would be asking us who we had been sitting next to in school that day. She would examine our heads for hours and our eyes would be watering by the time she had finished. It was a terrible ordeal and we all used to dread it! We were all happy enough to go through these rituals though as we had heard some terrible rumours at school about kids not having much food to eat or even being molested and treated badly by their parents. We were fortunate though and my Mam always made sure we had plenty to eat and decent clothes to wear, which made our home always a place of happiness. The only exception to this was when our old fella came home from the alehouse with a belly full of ale and put a dampener on everything with his drunken attitude.

We were always told to sit, as close as we could to the fire on those cold mornings to keep warm and there was always a large plate of toast to eat. The toast was cut in thick slices, with a big long handled knife from a real loaf, and then toasted on the open fire with my ma holding each round of bread with a table fork right up to the fire making sure it was nice and brown from the soaring heat. If we were lucky, sometimes there would be real butter to spread on it instead of the usual margarine or dripping. I remember the name of the margarine we had was called Snipe or

Echo. Looking back it was a horrible taste, but because of the war everything nice was rationed and hard to get hold of. We would still just wolf it down while it was hot, and then 'leg it' to school in case we were late, with me at the front hurrying my brothers along.

Taking my three brothers to school that day was very painful for me. My body was aching all over after the beating I had taken last night ' from my father. The lashings I got from his leather belt were bad enough, but where he had booted me in the leg was the most painful. The top of my thigh ached so much I could hardly walk properly. When my brothers and I finally arrived at the school gates I said my 'goodbyes' to them and I promised them faithfully that I would come and visit them. But, I told them that by then I would have my own horse, and if they behaved themselves, I would let each of them have a ride on it! Their faces beamed back at me in eager anticipation.

I had arranged to be at the gypsy camp for nine o'clock. That was the time when Rowena and the rest of the gypsies were departing, and I had promised I would definitely be there on time. I had walked about 50 yards or so past our school, incidentally I had to walk, as I didn't want to arouse any suspicion. If any of the teachers had seen me running away it would have certainly have brought it 'bang on top for me' and given the game away! When I eventually reached the main highway going in the direction of Knowsley, towards the gypsy camp pleasant thoughts came racing through my head. I was well out of sight from school by this time and I knew I was safe enough to start running without drawing attention to myself. So I set off at a pace 'this is the way to the gypsy camp... that's where Rowena is... that's where the horses are... that's where the caravans are...' All these wonderful things were running through my little mind. Elation washed over me and I found myself getting excited again in a happy sort of way. I attempted to run but the pain in my leg was excruciating. I just couldn't run as fast as I usually did and resorted to doing a kind of hop skip and jump alongside the big main road.

I also knew that it was well past nine o'clock as I had heard the school bell being rung in the playground some ten minutes ago. One of the teachers would always stand punctually every morning and at precisely nine o'clock ring a large brass hand bell. The second it stopped ringing every kid in that playground would have to stand very still and be very quiet, because woe betide you if you happened to move or talk! Discipline was very strict and if you happened to get caught out you would be punished - either by having to write out a couple of hundred lines after class had finished or, worse still, you would get the dreaded cane!

But I won't be getting the cane any more or told what to do; I've sacked all that, because where I am going I will be well out of it. I tried to hurry my pace along the road but I had to stop several times because of the pain in my wounded leg. Another thought crossed my mind - I wouldn't have to face my Dad any more! He wouldn't be giving me any more hidings! The thought of Rowena and running away with her spurned me on. I had less than a mile to go before I reached the camp - not long now I told myself. I knew I was well over half an hour late, but in just another ten minutes or so I had turned into the narrow country lane, bordered with tall hedgerows. This was the last bit of my hurried journey to the gipsy camp.

I knew this lane so well! After all I had been running up and down here for the past few weeks, every bend and hedgerow was familiar to me. After this long painful run I was completely shattered but I knew I had finally made it and a surge of happiness came over me. I had one smaller bend to turn and then I would be in there.

When I got around the bend I stopped suddenly in my tracks. I couldn't believe what I was seeing across the meadow. The gypsy camp had gone. It had completely vanished as though it had never been there. I was totally gutted, but more than that, I was so bewildered as to where they could have gone? I knew I was late - possibly half an hour at the most but I refused to believe that Rowena wouldn't wait for me! After a few minutes the reality hit home. She had gone with the rest of the gypsies. I never cry. Even when I got caned in school or when my old feller gave me a good hiding. But this was too much for me; I just broke down sobbing my heart out. After all I was just a little kid, what else could I do. I did contemplate at one stage quickly stealing a bike from somewhere and trying to catch up with them but I was knackered and it was beyond my physical capabilities. I felt so alone and desolate.

I think when a child gets a big disappointment in life, especially the way I did, it sort of does something to you. Rowena leaving without me had a profound effect on me. Initially it took me a long time to believe what had happened and it made me unwilling ever to put my trust in anyone ever again. I knew I would eventually have to go home and face the music and get what was coming to me. There is one thing for sure, that experience made me hard.

Hard as nails, and I don't mean that just in the fighting sense - but I became a kid that could survive on the streets of Liverpool, living only on my wits, doing a bit of this and a bit of that.

1940

I was born on the 7th April 1940 at 59 Barkbeth Road, Huyton Liverpool 14. I came into the world slap bang in the middle of the war that was ravaging the entire country. Germany was battering the cities of Britain. My three younger brothers came right after me William, James and Joseph. Those of us born between 1940 and 1945 were called 'war babies'.

One of my first memories is when I was twelve to eighteen months old and I remember being carried into an air raid shelter at the bottom of our garden. Incidentally, I have heard that the medical profession have evidence that some people can actually remember being born and their turbulent journey out of the womb, let alone the first sounds of their own screaming voices. I don't know if this is true or just a very vivid imagination as some people cant even remember if they have tied their own shoe laces before leaving the house. Now I personally can't remember being born myself, but I do remember being wrapped in a big grey blanket and being taken into the shelter. I can recall somebody's voice saying "Pass the baby over here luv." and then being cradled on that person's knee. It was a weird feeling and there were huge green candles standing tall, spread all about the shelter ready to be lit at the start of the blackout. The shelter was made of tin and iron corrugated sheets bolted together to form an arch shaped tunnel above the ground. Every household had access to one, as this was the only protection you had from the bombings. I will never forget the sirens that were used to warn of imminent air raids and to give the all clear that meant you could come out of your shelter and get on with life. The same sirens were later used in the 1950's for the local factories to mark the start of shifts and signify when it was time to 'knock off'. It was only when I was four or five that I understood what the dreadful noises were and the significance of the bombings and sirens. As Liverpool was a large shipping port it got a lot of the Germans attention during the war years, and the Bootle docks seemed to be a constant target, seen to be of major importance for its shipping trade and docks. Liverpool like London and other major cities had a terrible time, but being a kid a lot of the atrocity passed me by. When the war ended we had a big street party to celebrate VE day. As there were not many cars about in those days the whole street dragged as many tables and chairs out into the middle of the road as they could muster, and hung union jack flags on stretched out strings from one house to another on opposite sides of the street. There wasn't much food as times were hard still but everybody pitched in. Knowing my Mam she would have made sure we were well looked after, with a couple of chocolate biscuits or a slice of cake on our plates to make it extra special. Somebody had made a life-size Hitler out of old clothes and papers, which was paraded about on a long pole while the onlookers cheered and clapped. This manikin was later to be thrown on top of the big bonfire that was being built at the end of the street. When he went up in flames that night everybody started singing and cheering. This was followed by all the grown ups dancing to their stupid music in the street.

There were some terrible goings on during the war in our street, like every street in the city most likely, with some terrible fights and arguments. Most of the fights were neighbours accused of 'carrying on' with people they shouldn't have, mainly as they were living for the day, not knowing if they were going to live or die. Two married women who lived just across the road were never away from the Yankee air force camp, which was not far from where we lived. They used to come home at night and throw wild parties with white American soldiers and sometimes black, coming and going at all hours. There were some ferocious fights between black and white American soldiers. Most of the fighting would be over a white British girl who had been playing about with both sides of the racial split. All while their poor husbands were probably dying in the trenches abroad. It was terrible! I believe though that when the husbands came back a lot of their wives were pregnant even though it was slap in the middle of the war and their husbands hadn't been home for months. Wally Mitchell was the only black kid in our school; he was born in the middle of the war too. We didn't treat him any different then as we didn't know anything about racism and he was just accepted as one of us, and even though the adults may have seen it as a bad thing I cant recall anybody sneering on his family or looked down their noses at him.

People were still struggling after the war, as there was still not a lot to go around. As things were so bad and on ration, people used to help each other out borrowing cups of sugar, a bit of margarine or a loaf of bread until pay day even lending each other bags of coal to keep a struggling household warm. The culture was to just help one another out. People were always knocking on our door to beg and borrow goods. My mother had just sold a thriving fish and chip shop business and we were doing well. It was considered a big thing to own your own business at that time and my parents had moved to our new house in Huyton just before I was born. Some kids were still in a bad way though, running around with no shoes on and the arses of their kecks torn. I used to stand by our gate and watch the gangs of kids coming down to get their free meal from the dinner centre. They always walked in neat lines with their free meal tickets clutched firmly in their hands the teachers or masters walking at the side of them carried a sort of cane like keeping the kids in tow, those teachers looked real evil bastards to me. I was in awe of these street kids and wanted to be one of them. It was just like something out of Oliver Twist with these kids queuing up in the street to get a terrible meal of 'Pom' which was a powdered mash potato substance served with a bit of gravy and a round of bread, if they were lucky! This was probably the only meal that they had during the day, as there often wasn't even a stick of furniture or lino (a form of floor covering) in some of their houses due to the poverty they were enduring. Nobody had heard of such a thing as a carpet, it was just lino on the floor with a homemade rug if you were fortunate enough to have enough old patches of cloth and the course sacking that was needed to make one. This was of course the carpet of the day; if you didn't have any lino then some proud women would have spotlessly clean scrubbed floorboards on show. It proves one thing; just because some people were poor it didn't mean that they couldn't still be clean. It didn't cost a lot for a bar of soap! By the way this 'Pom' was how we English got the name Pommies, mainly given to us by the Australian soldiers.

We were fortunate though as my dad was one of the bosses on the docks and there was always goodies coming into the house. My three older brothers also used to come home from sea with an Aladdin's hoard of treasures that you just couldn't get hold of at home. It was unbelievable the things they brought home to sell, and our house used to burst with black-market contraband stock. There weren't many cars about but the ones I saw all seemed to stop at our house and the visitors would leave with nice rugs, furniture and all sorts of fashionable accessories. I know times were said to be hard during the war but I lived a life of luxury as a small child. On my seventh birthday I was given a silver scooter with red wheels, most of the other kids were playing with a wheel and stick, running alongside them in the roads trying to keep them moving. When I played on my scooter the other kids used to ask "Go on Charlie give us a go, give us a go" and they would all end up queuing to have a go on my scooter, what a time!

Before the great D day invasion my older brothers came home on leave from sea and my Ma dressed me and Billy up in two little white US Navy sailor suits that they had bought for us while they were in America, they even had little whistles hanging off the jackets secured to the lapels by a small platted rope. We were only about four and two years of age when my older sister Delia took us down to the Liverpool docks, the river Mersey was chock a block with battleships all flying flags and banners, to meet her future husband wearing these suits. He was a sailor called Joey Hanson and my sister was only about eighteen. There were loads of American service men in the city at that time all getting prepared for the invasion and while we were on the docks in these gleaming white sailor outfits out of nowhere all these Yanks came up "Gee look at these kids" They started taking photographs but me and Billy didn't really understand what it was all about but when they started patting us on the heads and giving us bars of chocolate, we were made up. It must have been a big moral boost for the Yanks seeing us British kids in their colours especially since they had come into the war after us.

Our neighbours were odd too; Richard Jones (Dick) and his wife Mary Jones lived next door to us with their son Dickie. Dickie was a bit retarded and a real crazy lad. Sometimes this kid would come in to our house and play with me. My mother must have felt sorry for him, but sometimes I would end up alone with him in the street or back garden unbeknown to my Ma, and if caught I would be dragged back inside. She never scolded him though. I would only have been about for or five and didn't realise, I was in the hands of a raving lunatic. Only my Ma would have known that; even the kid himself didn't know he was mad. I remember the day the men in the white coats came to his house for him and they took that poor kid away screaming, I never saw him again! You would never see any deformed or backwards kids running about the streets in those days, they were all taken away and put in a home somewhere. I never saw a kid in a wheelchair all the time I was growing up, you just never saw them, not like today when they are well looked after and loved. Some of the kids were taken away from their families and even their own parents never saw them again. I heard some terrible things about what happened to them and how they were treated. The three divisions across the British nation of Upper, Middle and Lower classes were rigid and everybody knew their place, bowing down when they had to. Which I think was totally wrong.

There were some funny things that happened too, along side the sad times. A lot of households used to keep the odd hen and chicken in their back gardens to ensure they had some real eggs to eat. This was to replace the horrible powdered eggs that was all you could buy in the shops, but for some reason we had our own cockerel as well. It was a big Rhode Island cockerel that resembled an Eagle, and to us kids it looked like a monster with huge steel talons. It was a horrible sight! In our house we had to go outside to use the 'lavie', it was a proper toilet with electricity and all modern facilities but it just happened to be accessed via the back yard. Well every time you went outside this huge cockerel, that as a kid appeared to be up to my shoulder in size, would chase you with its neck stuck out and feathers all haunched up. The only thing we could do was to take the yard sweeping brush with us. It had a long handle on it and would allow us to keep the bird at bay while we legged it to the other door and shut it behind us fast, still holding on to that brush for safety. At that time all the women used to clean their houses meticulously. If they didn't and they ignored the council's rules, which were very strict in those years, then they would end up getting thrown out of their houses, as the council inspector would take their homes off them for being kept dirty. It didn't take much for the council to evict you and you would just find your furniture piled up on the small front garden of the house where you 'used to' live. Anyway one afternoon while Mrs Jones was happily singing a little tune, as all the women did while working, and scrubbing her back kitchen step, our cockerel got over the joining garden fence, it must have been about a meter high. She must have been kneeling down with her arse stuck up in the air and the backs of her bare legs exposed. The bastard cockerel must have gone stalking her and she didn't see it coming, so when it got close enough up to her...BANG it had her! My Mam was out in the back hanging out some washing when all of a sudden she heard a lot of commotion and the high-pitched scream. Mrs Jones started shouting in a high piercing voice "Dick, Mr Seiga's cock has just pecked my arse. Dick, Dick, quick! It's Mr Seiga's cock - its got hold of me." Well my ma couldn't stop laughing and almost fell over the washing line.

The other neighbours were characters too; take Flo Charlesworth my sister's friend who lived on her own a few doors away down our road. Her father was in the army serving abroad and her mother had run away with a Yank. When the war was raging and the black outs were on, the two of them used to lay either side of me on an old mattress on the floor, and to stop themselves and me getting too scared they would start to sing all the songs of the time to try and keep their fear at bay, I clearly recall them singing White Cliffs of Dover to me while we all lay down trembling. There was also the Peters family; they were a large family who always appeared to be very poor. Even though the father was blind he had a huge pigeon shed in his back garden, and years later when my brother got in trouble with the police he would hide in that pigeon shed to escape being caught when the coppers knocked on our door. It wasn't just him hiding there though; all the military deserters would be taking refuge in PeeO's pigeon shed too. PeeO was his nickname and everybody knew his family and the hideout in his back garden. They all used to make a beeline for it when they were in trouble and needed somewhere to hide. There were that many people kipping in there with the pigeons that PeeO kept adding on to the building, until he had no garden left and it was just one big pigeon shed. Every council street had a set of council house snobs and in our street it was the Harrison's. They were the neighbourhood Tories and their son was the only kid on the street to join the boy scouts and play in bands. Every Sunday all the bands would play on parade to celebrate events such as empire day, with brass bugles and big bass drums. It was unbelievable to see as a kid, and we all used to chase behind them as they marched down the roads. The Harrison's were trying to be middle class but they were only working class like the rest of us. They walked about trying to be something their not with their heads in the air like Walter Mitties thinking they are above everybody else. In the lower class areas we were supposed to have know our place and the rules we had to abide by, even though we still tried to rebel against them. When the councillors came round in their little vans or cars campaigning for votes with a loud speaker tied on top people showed their true colours. If the Tory's down our street they would get verbal abuse and a good slagging off from everyone they passed even the kids let fly with abuse if there were no coppers about to keep the peace. If there were bizzies with the councillors then of course we would all have to be quiet and know our place. The Labour car got cheered and clapped with everybody rallying round. The working class people at that time were more clannish than anybody, helping one another out with a neighbour always being there for you ready to lend a hand. The Harrison's couldn't see the value in this keeping their doors shut, never socialising with anybody. You would see them walking to church on Sunday with their noses in the air ignoring the rest of us but deep down they looked like they needed a good pan of scouse down them. They were all built like beanpoles looking pale and drawn. Later on in years one of the Harrison sons joined the prison service and became a screw, so that says it all.

During the blackouts when it was pitch black, there were a lot of indecent assaults and rapes of women. So because of this some women started wearing slacks as a form of deterrent on their way to work at the ammunition factory during the blackouts. To some of the ordinary working class men this was seen as a total lack of respect and an insult. Only the men wore trousers in the house and certainly not the women. This would be used as a form of ridicule in the alehouse, like the old saying goes 'what's up? Is she wearing the trousers in your house then or you?' My Mam thought she would get a pair of slacks too, not wanting to take a chance if she didn't need to while going about her business in the dark. Especially as a fiend nicknamed the 'Glosher Man' was carrying out a series of indecent assaults on vulnerable women at the time. He used to wear creepers, a type of baseball shoe, and he would creep up behind women in the dark and put his hands up their skirts before they even knew the predator was there. My old fella who always wanted to be one of the lads was sat in our house rotten drunk; he had been out on a bender and was still bladderd, when my Ma appeared wearing her slacks. It was like showing a red flag to a bull. He kicked off good style on her "What are you doing wearing them pants in this house? I'm the only one wearing pants here not you!" and he literally got hold of my mother and started cutting the pants off her with a cut throat open razor. As he was doing it in his drunken state he slashed my mothers legs. He was a right bastard! Another time my sister asked my Ma to accompany her on a date with a Yank called Isaac from the Deep South. He was a tall Texan fella and at the time was in the US air force as a pilot. She was seeing him that night but she was a bit shy having only just met him and so asked my Ma to go along and chat to his mate just for company. Our Delia liked the Yanks, as they were all well mannered and polite. I remember myself the big tall Texan Delia was courting saying "How do ma'am" and tugging his hat to my Ma whenever he came into our house. As well as this they all had gleaming white teeth and were always chewing gum, unlike most British people who by the time they were in their mid thirties had a full set of false teeth, due to the lack of calcium and bad food. False teeth must have been a good business to have been in at that time you know. My Mam went along to say hello and introduce herself, with the aim of getting home again as soon as she could. Of course you were ostracized by the married women if you were seen talking to the Yanks and were married yourself. Unfortunately my Mam and Delia were spotted and it gets back to my old fella dead quick. So he has gone fuckin' berserk, he has got a spade and is digging my Mam a grave in the back garden waiting for her to come home! Some time later my sister Delia got a letter from the air force base saying Isaac had been killed in action somewhere above Germany, she was due to fly out to America and marry him, so she was totally devastated. I believe it took her a long time to get over it.

My old fella wanted it all his own way at times and always kept my mother down. It was like the pot calling the kettle black, it even goes on today in some families. These women are intimidated and are scared to stand up for themselves worried about the severe consequences that may follow. He was a very vain man and used to wear a pin stripe suit with collar, tie and trilby hat all the time, thinking he looked the part. I will never forget as long as I live that whenever he was going out with a parcel in his hand he would look at me and say "Come on Charlie get your coat on your coming with me for a walk." He would always go out when it was dark in the blackout and I could never understand why he wanted me to go with him; he never gave me a sweet or anything. He wasn't a proper dad to his kids, as my Mam used to look after us and give us presents, never him, which made this even stranger. We would walk along and if we happened to come across a couple of coppers on the beat he would hold my hand and in a gentle loving voice say, "Don't be frightened son, just look at the stars and think happy thoughts. It will all be alright I'm here to look after you." The coppers of course would see us and think what a loving and affectionate father and son, and we would never be asked any questions. When they had passed by the affection would stop and it would be back to "Hurry up and stop dawdling will you kid." This was all to ensure we wouldn't get stopped, what with him carrying stolen property he had received ready for selling later on at the end of our walk. One trip was to a big house and all the way there my old fella was carrying a bag. I could hear noises coming from the bag that sounded like a clock chiming 'ding dong, ding dong'. I was saying "Where's that noise coming from Dad, I think I can hear a clock." "Nowhere. Your just imagining it and don't be shouting that out." he said in a gruff voice. "But Dad I can hear a clock." "You can hear nothing your imagining it, keep quiet." When we got to the house and knocked on the door a woman opened it, she threw her arms around him and gave him a big kiss. I was taken inside and sat on a chair in the corner. He put the bag down on the floor and pulled out this big magnificent golden clock. He carefully put it on the table and said, "There what do you think of that then?" "Oh Fred, Fred its beautiful" and then she gave him another big kiss. I wasn't even patted on the head or anything just given something to play with while they both disappeared for a bit of the other upstairs before we would head off back home. He had a different attitude on the way back home. I was allowed to run about and be myself, as he now had nothing to worry about.

I started school in 1945 just after the war, when I was five years of age. I think everybody remembers their first day at school. A lot of kids crying for their Ma's, as they didn't want to be left, and everyone making a big fuss. I wasn't bothered though and by the end of the first day I had made a load of mates. All the kids in the gang of lads were from around my own neighbourhood and we had a great time. Some of these kids are still my friends today. On my first day at Longview school, my Mam had made me some butties cut up small and had put them in a red tin oxo box with the lid held on tight with an elastic garter ready for me to carry. My Mam used to put an apple in my tin for the teacher and as they were very hard to get hold of it was used as a sort of bribe to ensure I could eat my own butties and not have to eat the school food, which she knew was of a very poor standard. Gruel and foul tapioca pudding like frogspawn, which made kids vomit just by looking at it wasn't good enough for me. I had been brought up on good clean food and I wasn't going to be allowed to eat that crap. Longview was a nice school and I did great there, eventually our Billy and my other brothers joined me and proved themselves there too. Although both my parents were catholic, my old man wanted us to go to a good protestant school like Longview. This was so that half our time wasn't spent praying and saying Hail Mary's and we would get a better standard of education.

The families on both sides of my bloodline were completely different, even though as I have said, both families were Catholic and staunch Catholics at that. My mother's family were what we would call, 'Tuppenny Toffs' and when they did lower themselves to visit us in Huyton we would all have to be on our best behaviour. Not running around or being seen as unruly kids. We were instructed to show good manners at the table as we sat down to eat with them and this would have gone well, except none of us knew how to use cutlery properly or not put our elbows on the table. We also had to try and pronounce our H's properly and my Mam used to correct us and make us repeat how every word should sound. We all knew it was just a 'put on' for my Mam's side of the family but we didn't want to show her up and every one of us tried our best. My Mam's parents were quite well off and made a living in both the car renovation business and in the food catering business, owning a food warehouse in the South side of the city supplying groceries of all shapes and sizes to the smaller shops in the area. They lived in a large house in Parliament Street, located in the South End of the city close to their warehouse, and that big house looked so beautiful to us kids. My Mam used to tell us stories about the house, how it was spotlessly clean and how the many steps leading up to the big Georgian house along with the brass nameplate were scrubbed and polished every day. All the kids from that house, except my Mam, ended up in good careers and marrying 'good stock'. One of my Mam's sisters became the Headmistress at Notre Dame School for Girls in Liverpool. Uncle Charlie had a top job in the government of South Africa and Aunty Bell had large premises in Australia that she moved to with her well to do husband. They were all quite wealthy people in their own way. I also had an uncle on that side of the family that went by the name of 'Shanghai Brown'. He was seen as the black sheep of the family! He owned a bed and breakfast boarding house near the docks and had a good trade from seamen and travellers alike.

He got his nickname as he used to slip his guests 'Mickey Fins' to drug them and when they awoke they would find themselves on a sailboat signed up for a two-year or more journey.

Of course on the other side of my bloodline my Dad's family were all real 'scallies'. They were a big family of brothers who were always found fighting and lived down the South End in Beaufort Street, which was considered a real bad slum area at that time. The houses were all small two up and two downs, with no toilets or running water. Their lives were bad and poverty was hard so they all ended up going away to sea to make a living and get out of the slums. Most of them joined the 'Merch' our name for the Merchant Navy when we were kids. Everybody wanted to go away to sea; it was just the done thing. They were just a different class of family all together from my Mam's side. My Mothers name was Jane Brown and my father was Fredrico Seiga.

When my old fella was thirteen he joined the Merch himself taking after his own father and brothers. The lure of the sea and the opportunity to see the world and its delights, apart from leaving the hardship of Liverpool, must have been uncontrollable even though it was known to be a hard life at sea. It was a few years later when he returned to Liverpool that he met my mother in a dance hall and they hit it off straight away. My mother's parents didn't approve at all of his background and thought he wasn't good enough for my Ma. They often told her that as a sixteen year old that young love was blind but she just couldn't see the bad in him for her youth. Her parents could see him for what he was though and his trendy clothes and flash appearance didn't fool them at all. This didn't stop my Ma as she had a strong head on her shoulders and they were soon a courting couple. Knowing her parents didn't approve saying he would be gallivanting off to sea all the time and leaving her alone, the couple decided to marry in secret. The only way this was possible was to get married quickly in a registry office, which they knew if found out would break their parents hearts as they both sets would expect a traditional Catholic church wedding. Once they were married they still couldn't tell anyone what they had done for fear of what would happen and so lived a secret life, both returning to their parents home of a night time and pretending to still be a courting couple. My Ma told me years later how much she loved him and that love really did blind her. The priests of the time used to dress in long black cloaks and carry long staffs, they were intimidating people always asking their flock for donations to the church. Even though the members of their parish could be starving, they always lived well, often having large wine cellars in their big houses, which they enjoyed with the chosen few. The Catholic priests had a good relationship with the local registrars and if a Catholic couple got married in secret the priest would always find out. Most secret marriages were due to an unplanned pregnancy and childbirth out of marriage was seen as a major sin. Of course my parents marriage was discovered and the priest confronted my mothers parents. He shamed both families into having a second church wedding, done this time the right way. My mother was accused by that priest of being pregnant and carrying a bastard, but she was actually still a virgin and had never consummated her marriage with her new husband.

When my mother's father passed away, the family wealth was distributed amongst the surviving family and my Ma bought a fish and chip shop with her slice, she must have inherited along with the wealth a good business head from her father. My old fella wanted to spend the cash on flash living and would have soon squandered it away!

But enough about my family history and back to my childhood where at my home everything was going well, we had a smashing school, great family, a nice warm house; we were happy and wanted for nothing with all the best toys. I used to like playing with the older 'make do' toys as well, such as 'steeries' ~ steering carts made from old pram wheels and a tied on rope to steer it at the front. We used to play hopscotch, rounders and other street games as well as having a swing that hung off one of the streets lampposts. The girls would play skipping with a long rope covering the whole width of the road. They would often sing skipping songs in unison as they played. Anything new was exciting to us and when one day my uncle Charlie came to visit us driving a Triumph Mayflower car and all the kids were gathered round it looking at this car as if it was gold. They had never seen anything like it.

Then out of the blue tragedy hit our house and from that moment on my young life changed forever!

1950

I remember that day vividly, coming out of school 'happy as Larry' with my three brothers and my friends. Bobby Mitchell, Tucker Ferris and John Pollock my best mates from my class, all lived around the corner from me and as a gang we merrily made our way home. As my brothers and I walked into the house I saw it was crowded with all sorts of strange men. They all seemed to be wearing long trench coats or macs with large brown or green trilby hats. They looked so out of place in our house and for a moment I thought it was the school board, but then slowly realised there were just too many on them for it to be about us kids. My Mam was sat sobbing and called us to her before cuddling us and holding us tight. The men were ransacking the house, pulling draws open and tipping our beloved belongings onto the floor. The house was in turmoil and our privacy was being invaded. I couldn't believe what was happening as our house was getting properly turned over by these men. By this time both my brothers and I were crying too, begging my mother to tell us what was happening. It turned out that two of my older brothers, who were both at least ten years older than me, had been involved in an armed robbery and these men were bizzies searching for evidence.

My brothers and their friend Benny Nolan had found that a popular tailor in the city was taking a lot of money from the sailors returning from sea spending their well earned pay offs. It was a large shop specialising in flashy shirts and suits that the sailors would wear to impress the local girls. My brothers and their mate thought that it would be a walk over to take his money. They were all home from sea themselves, but now the war was over the work from the docks was drying up and their money was running out too. I learned later that they had no experience in robberies but had been practicing in their bedrooms when my Ma was out, hiding their faces with black neckerchiefs and talking in voices that would put the fear of Christ into the man they were going to rob. They didn't have a clue how to commit an armed robbery but were determined to have it away. The plan was that one of my brothers, Freddy, would enter the shop with Benny and hold the tailor hostage. My brother would threaten the tailor with a gun they had acquired while Benny tied him up tight with ropes. They would then make off with the cash getting shut of the gun and clothes they were wearing to my other brother who would be waiting across the road. The plan wasn't too bad, except Benny had taken a cosh with him and got a bit carried away knocking fuck out of the poor tailor and putting him in a really bad way. They managed to get the cash and escape without getting caught, even giving their blood stained clothes and gun to Eddie my eldest brother waiting outside. The two of them then made their way home as fast as they could. Well the robbery became headline news and the use of a gun made the robbery a very unusual and vicious crime. The bizzies were everywhere looking for suspects and the whole city knew what had happened. Later on they came badly unstuck due to my dopey brother Eddie. Instead of getting shut of the gun and clothes in the river Mersey or having the sense to burn the clothes somewhere out of the way, he took them to work with him, where by now he was late for his shift. He put the bag in the bottom of his locker and went to work. What he didn't remember was that another bloke on the next shift shared his locker, and when the shift changed the man found the bag of blood stained clothes and a gun sticking out of it. It was after all just staring him in the face!

The bizzies soon arrested my brother and Herbert Balmer the top policeman of the day grilled him for hours. He was ruthless and as corrupt as they come by fabricating evidence and lying in court to get his captives sent down. Our kid wouldn't give his brother and friend away, even after getting a good beating in the cells. So the coppers tried a different avenue and went to visit his wife. They told her what he had done and forced her to tell them who his friends were. She told them he always knocked around with his brother Freddy and Benny Nolan who lived in Huyton and that they were always together. Soon realising her mistake she contacted my Ma before the bizzies could arrive and told her everything that had happened. My poor Ma was completely taken by surprise and badly shaken over it all! But being a good mother who would do anything for her sons, including if required giving up her own life, decided to help. She confronted Freddy who immediately tells her the full story; none of us could ever lie to her! She got advice from a trusted friend who knew far more about the bizzies procedures than my Ma, who herself, didn't know a thing about the ways of the law. She went round to Benny Nolan's house to warn him and told him to say nothing at all to the coppers, as they had no evidence to connect them both to the crime. Benny was weak though and under interrogation told Herbert Balmer everything, including that fact that my mother had warned him of their expected arrival and her advice to say nothing. He was meant to be a loyal mate to my brothers, what a prick he turned out to be.

Later in court Benny Nolan practically got a walk over for helping out the bizzies receiving only three years in a borstal young offenders institute. My eldest brother Eddy received five years for assisting the robbery but Frederick, who was only nineteen years of age, was sent down for ten years penal servitude for using a loaded gun. Herbert Balmer had played the court well, saying that Frederick was the leader of the gang and that the tailor was lucky not to have been shot dead by the loaded gun, which allegedly had a very sensitive trigger. Gun crime was almost unheard of and the punishment dished out by the courts was severe.

Things soon went from bad to worse when my only remaining older brother Ged was caught for some other robbery and also given three years in jail. He had fallen in with the wrong crowd and thought he could bring some easy money into the household.

After this all our lives changed and the local community started to shun our family. Many people who we thought were family friends disappeared and some of my mates were told not to play with me. This is where true loyalties are tested; there were a few neighbours who were still friends to our Ma and us kids. Take Mrs Connell who lived a few doors away, a hard-working woman who had a nice clean home. Her children still played with me and her daughter Janette is still a friend of mine today. A compassionate woman, Mrs Connell helped my Ma out here and there. There were also the Stewarts, they were good decent people too and of course the PeeO's who like ourselves were poor and had fuck all, but at least they didn't blank us. Delia my sister had moved out and was living her own life with her new husband and we hit rock bottom. I knew my Ma had sold everything we owned to pay the legal fees to help my brothers' court cases and we were now poverty stricken ourselves. During school my younger brothers and I were soon clutching our own free meal tickets, and standing at the back of the dinner queue. This is all while the other kids, who were once our mates were at the front of the queue ridiculing us. My dad started drinking heavily, and was soon to be frequenting the alehouse even more so. I remember he never seemed to have the bottle to help in any way and left it all to my poor Ma to sort out. So me and my other innocent young brothers were accused of anything bad that happened in the neighbourhood and every petty crime was blamed on us.

BLAME THE SEIGAS

My Ma and what was left of our family were tired of hearing "It was probably those Seigas again". Every time something got stolen either from a house, a toy from the street or an item from school me and my brothers were wrongly accused. We became outcasts in the community where we lived and the teachers at school looked down at us. I hated the fuckin' lot of them. I started to dread going to school from then, on but had no choice and took my brothers every day. There were times I started thinking about sagging off but still had to do as I was told and worried about the consequences of being found out. This was just the way my Ma had brought us all up, knowing right from wrong. She would say to me every morning "Take care of them Charlie, you're the oldest and strongest now" meaning my younger brothers of course. There was a bit of bullying going on at school but I could handle myself and always made sure that nobody touched my younger brothers. She used to tell me to keep out of trouble, as she didn't want the police knocking on the door again. Day and night I had it drummed in to me as she was dreading anything happening to us all, or us taking after my older brothers. After getting all this preaching off my Ma I eventually told her what had been going on and how the teachers were treating us, always looking down their noses at us. I told her everything including how it was particularly bad at dinner times getting ridiculed in the queue and the state of the school meals. As she had more dignity and pride than anyone else I know, she started giving us four pennies each to buy some dinner with instead of eating at school. I don't know where she got the money from as there wasn't a bean in the house and she would be out all day at work and couldn't provide dinner for us herself. "Go easy on the money Charlie" she would say "make sure you get something down yous till I get home from work"

So it began, every lunch time at school me and my brothers would pretend to be going home from school to eat, which would of course be all lies. We would instead all go to the local shops and I soon learnt to economise with the four pence each we had. I would then start to do the daily shopping, this was something as a kid I had never done in my life before. I would try and balance the money out and get enough to go round. Especially on a winters day when it would be important to try and get something hot for us all. You used to be able to buy broken biscuits a lot cheaper than normal packets. So I would buy two penneth of broken biscuits at Gourley's ~ which was a well known established grocers around that time, then go next door to Waterworths the fruit and veg shop and buy one or two pennyworths of fades, which were bruised apples or pears. Usually it would be the sour green English apples as we were not usually lucky enough to get pears. What was left over was spent on a Vienna long loaf saving just enough to go to the chippy. Of course we couldn't afford a lot else by now so I would buy just one bag of chips but if my budget was tight it would be a penny bag of scraps. These were the left over bits of crispy fried batter that had been made while frying fish or any other leftovers. We would break the Vienna open, scooping out the middle. We would then fill it back up with the chips or the scraps and leg it to a secluded field out of the way of prying eyes ready for our feast. We would each take turns to have a bite passing the loaf around. Incidentally all shops were known in their own right at that time as there was no such thing as supermarket and price wars had never been heard of.

On returning to school we would make out that we had been home for dinner and been sat by the fire in our house enjoying a right good meal, but of course it was all just lies to save face to our mates.

In 1952 we had a Christmas party at school and we were all told to take some food in to school to fill the party table. In our class of about twenty we were asked to help make hats and paper decorations made of coloured paper strips looped together to make long streamers. The teachers closing words were "Don't forget to ask your parents what you can bring in to make our class party the best. We want to beat the other classes don't we?" I had told my Ma that we needed to take something in, but as we were on the bread line and my brothers needed something to take in too it was very difficult. She managed to scrape something together out of the pantry for my three brothers before she rushed off to work. That left my old fella to try and sort me out with something to take. He knew we didn't get on and wasn't too bothered about helping me, but after a bit of nagging him and me telling him what it was like at school he said, "What the fuck do you want me to do about it? I've got nothing and can't do anything." Well anything would be better than nothing I persisted, as I didn't want to be left out. So he went to the pantry and pulled out a half loaf and got himself the long handled bread knife. He roughly cut some rounds ready to slap some margarine and cheap meat paste on them to make some sandwiches. As he cut the uneven rounds he managed to cut his fuckin' finger and some of the blood went on the bread. He thought I hadn't seen it and as I didn't want a crack over the back of my head I stood silently waiting. He slyly put the bread with the blood on it in the middle and covered it up fast with the marg and paste before quickly wrapping them up in a sheet of the Liverpool Echo newspaper as fancy paper just wasn't available in our house. So I wouldn't feel ashamed I ran upstairs and pulled out the big draw in my Ma's wardrobe, and used the brown draw lining paper to wrap the butties up again outside the Echo paper in a more respectable way. I found an old elastic garter to hold the paper tight just like my Ma had used on that oxo tin a few years earlier.

So when I arrived in school the food parcels were being put on the teachers big table, some wrapped in Christmas paper, some decorated with berries and some lovely big packages. The table looked fantastic, all colourful and bright. I felt ashamed of my offering and so kept it inside my jacket until close enough to the table to put it on and sneaked it amongst the other lovely packets. When we were all sat at our wooden desks the teacher came in and said "Now boys and girls lets see what you have all brought for our lovely party later on. This table looks fantastic, what a lovely spread." He started to pick them up one at a time. The first was a lovely cherry cake baked by one of the mothers, covered in icing with a little snowman to decorate the top. "Who brought this lovely cake?" Little Tommy at the back raised his hand "Me sir my mum made it special." "Very good Tommy give your mum my regards and thank her for such a lovely cake." Next to be assessed was a tin of mixed fruit, along with a tin of pears, both of which were real luxuries. "All the way from Africa, who brought these delicacies in?" Janet Smith said "Me sir, my dad brought them over for us. He's in the royal Navy." What a fuckin' game this was, I only had my butties. When eventually he got to my parcel, I was sinking lower and lower in my chair. I saw the look of disappointment and frown come over his face as he picked it up. As he pulled the garter away and snapped it open, the butties exploded all over the table. You could see the blood on two of the white butties as clear as day and the teacher just let out a noise of distaste and shook his head, all the time looking directly at me, before bundling my offering into the bin. He didn't ask who had sent them, he didn't need to as I was bright red with shame and he could only see my nose and eyes above the top of my desk.

Thinking about that later, he must have had some breeding in him not to ridicule me, as a lot of the other teachers would have done, given that opportunity. I admired him at the time for that. He let himself down though in a big way when the party itself started. When I went to take a piece of cake from the table he grabbed my arm and whispered to me "That's not yours Seiga" and then gave me one of them looks which stopped me taking anything off that table all day even though I was hungry and there was plenty to go around. That was the saddest Christmas I had ever experienced in my young life, and I knew then that no matter what happened from then on I would make sure I never had a Christmas like that again. So fuck the teachers and fuck that school with its pompous attitudes.

It wasn't just the school that had a problem with me either though. One of my mates Ralph Robinson who lived at no 59 Stockbrige Lane, no 59 was our house number too, invited me over to play and have tea. His house was in quite a posh area and when I walked in and saw real carpets on the floor it took me back to the life we used to have ourselves. Ralph wanted to be my best mate and thought I would protect him in the playground as he used to get bullied a bit. We played well together with his toys and his mum had even brought us a cup of hot Horlicks drink and a biscuit to keep us going. I could sense something had gone wrong as after a while of playing her attitude suddenly changed and she came to us saying, "I think your friend had better go home NOW!" I left not knowing what had happened with a puzzled Ralph shouting he would see me tomorrow as the door shut behind me. I think her friends had arrived and told her who I was and my family history, when they left she decided I wasn't good enough for Ralph to play with and threw me out. The next day in the playground Ralph kept his distance from me and when I challenged him he told me his mum had told him to stay away from me and that he couldn't play with me anymore.

Years later when I was a young man I went into a local dance hall and Ralph was in there with his mates calling over to me "Charlie, Charlie how's things?" He came running over to me and wanted to shake my hand. I was a professional criminal by then with a strong reputation and was living my life to the full with money, fast cars, nice clothes and plenty of women around me. You name it and I had it! He was still just a Liverpool zombie, clocking on and off a typical workhorse of the day, but he remembered me from when we were kids. He said to the work mates he was with from one of the local office blocks, "This is Charlie Seiga he's my best mate from school." I couldn't control myself with anger from all those years ago. I just looked at him and said "Ralph, I wasn't your best school mate. I thought I was, but I wasn't. You K-B'd me when I was just a kid and was wrongly accused of being a thief by your own fuckin' mother" (K-B'd meaning he had knocked me back). I just turned my back on him and walked away over the dance floor to my up and coming villain mates.

But anyway there we were getting ridiculed and blamed for every little misdemeanour that happened and times were getting harder and harder for us all. I was getting into more fights than soft Joe, just sticking up for my brothers and myself, but I was also becoming hard. Once me and my gang were playing in a field, climbing trees for conkers, when two coppers came over asking us to move on because the owners wanted us off their land. The coppers asked us all our names and addresses, mainly to scare us a bit, when my mates told them who they were one by one their response was always the same "Go on get home and don't be coming back round here again." When I told him the names of me and my brothers they were ready to take the Seiga brothers into Huyton police station just because of who we were ready to charge us with anything they could. They must have had second thought because after a while they sent us on our way calling after us "Get home you little bastards before we take you in".

Now in those days all the kids had to have a good haircut for school and long scruffy hair just wasn't allowed. The standard haircut for all kids was a short back and sides, not because this was the style we liked but because it would last longer before we needed another trip to the barbers. Barbers services were not cheap and it would cost six pence for a kid to get his haircut. For my brothers and me this was a small fortune.

The river Alt splits Huyton and on the other side of the Alt to where we lived were the 'Bootleites'. These were the kids that had been evacuated from Bootle in the North end of Liverpool right by the docks to Huyton where it was safer during the war. Their families were hard and the kids were hard too. They were our archenemies. If any of our crew went over the Alt on our own we would be chased and battered by the Bootleites and we would do the same to them if they came onto our turf. We used to have big battles with these kids who lived on the new purpose built estate on the other side of the Alt. The battles were vicious affairs with kids using anything they could get their hands on to have these violent kick-offs. Bottles, bricks, sods, sticks, catapults firing metal ball bearings or anything else we could find would be used in these ferocious confrontations. These battles happened regularly and the Alt was a permanent battleground for the kids that had suddenly been thrown together in quite a small environment. There were always shouts of "Get back to your own side!" or "Keep away from our yard. Otherwise yous will all get fuckin' done in!" before the fighting began.

Over the Alt in the Bootleites territory was a barber called 'Four Penny Jims' as the name suggests you could get a haircut there for four pence instead of the normal six pence. This was an opportunity none of our parents could ignore where every penny counts. He operated from his own council house where the kids would sit in his back kitchen, on an old chair with a sheet wrapped around their necks, ready for their cheap haircut. There were no frills in this place it was just like a sheep getting sheared. He would just tilt your head and get on with it, no messing around and quickly on to the next waiting kid. Now the Bootleites knew we all had to go for our haircuts here and would be waiting for us. The only way we could survive would be to go in a big gang and hope there was safety in numbers. If a kid decided to risk going alone you would often see him return with blood gushing from wounds where he had been hit by thrown stones or bricks or at best running for his life from a gang of pursuing kids. Running the gauntlet to get back across the Alt to your own patch was common often trying to jump across or wade and paddle across to get out of the way as quick as possible. The only bridge crossing at Woolfall Heath Avenue was too far to go when in a hurry!

My own research has shown me that Huyton itself is steeped in history, once being a dog-fighting village specialising in bulldog baiting. There is an old poem that sums the place up nicely 'Huyton Huyton two dogs fightin', one a black and one a white'un'. Incidentally a lot of villains emigrated from Huyton, Wyatt Earp and his family were born in Huyton with Roby, later going on to be gunslingers in the Wild West. The river Alt acquired its name from Viking days along with other local place names such as Kirkdale and Kirkby. The Vikings sailing up the Alt from Bootle and the river Mersey, taking what they pleased along the way, plundered Huyton. But that was hundreds of years ago now, wasn't it? Right now kids are fighting on both sides with short back and sides, wielding broken bottles and bricks in their hands, still having ago after all that time. I bet the Alt has many an untold secret from all those years ago, and the stories are still flowing down that river today, and will no doubt for years to come.

We used to make dams in the Alt and go swimming in it 'bollock'o', with us at one end and the Booltleites at the other. Somebody would eventually break the dam and then it would all kick off and there would be murder with all the kids fighting in the middle of the Alt. We all knew the score though and didn't go across the Alt if we didn't need to. I remember one time being on the run from them coming back from a hair cutting trip in a gang of about eight. We were outnumbered and knew we were going to get a good working over. We were legging it as fast as possible back to our own ground thinking we would be safe there, hurdling the Alt as far as we could. Some of us fell in the water panicking in our rush to get to the safety of the embankment our own side. We scrambled up it and looked back only to see these Bootleites coming across after us waving large sticks and other weapons shouting "get em, come on get em now!" We were terrified but all of a sudden I stopped in my tracks and told my mates to have a go back at them, but my mates were too scared. So I picked up a piece of broken roof slate from the ground. This big ginger haired fella was in the lead brandishing a hefty stick and charging towards us. As he got nearer and we realised we were all too done in to run any further I slung the slate at him. It was a perfect shot and slit his forehead wide open. There was blood spurting everywhere and this kid just fell to his knees in pain and started wailing. His screams were terrible and pierced the air, which by now had gone quite silent. His mates started panicking and turned to run back across the Alt. We started chasing after them picking up their discarded weapons to beat the fuck out of them. The ginger haired kid ended up in the local ozzy to sew together the big red gash he had acquired in his forehead. We were just going wild by now and the fighting was out of control, all down to the environment we were forced to live in and the hardships we faced.

It wasn't all misery though with the Bootleites and us nearly killing one another, my mates and me used to have some fun along the undulating embankment of the river Alt as well. I used to bunk off school to go there and be alone. Sometimes my mates would join me and we would have a boss time messing about in the Alt. Sometimes some of the girls we used to hang around with would sag off too and join us playing in the water by the Alt. I was coming up to my twelfth birthday, and at that age in life young boys start getting curious about the other lark, so I wanted to knock about with the girls too.

One girl in particular was always hanging about with us her name was Joan Yates. I didn't really know what life was all about then, I was only a kid and knew nothing about real sex, it was left to our own imaginations as we were never taught anything about that caper in school in those times. One day though I was left alone with Joan and found myself sat next to her as the others had wondered off further down the riverbank. We were just sitting in dead silence looking at the Alt but I knew I was expected to make a move on Joan. So I plucked up some courage and put my hand on her shoulder round her back as if I was cuddling her and didn't move an inch for ten minutes, we both just stared across the Alt. I knew I had to go further as Joan had a reputation for being a dirty little girl who liked to be groped and played with. So I started to edge my hand slowly down her front and eventually got my hand inside her jumper, I was really nervous and my heart was pumping at a pace. This is what old perves do nowadays and here I was a little kid with no experience of this before doing the same thing, slowly moving my hand towards her breast just praying she wouldn't stop me. She gave a little sigh, which I took as a sign to continue and put my hand on her breast. I couldn't believe, it I was actually touching a girls breast. I was saying to myself 'I can't believe this, I have actually got my hand on her tit'. I just didn't believe how far I had gone. I didn't move for about twenty minutes holding her breast in my hand not even massaging her, just rigid with fear. She was obviously disappointed that I hadn't done anything else, because she just gave a tut and said "Come on we will have to be getting off now!" and with that we both got up and went our separate ways. I ran back to my mates all excited ready to tell them what I had done and show them the hand that had touched a woman's breast. My mates who were all a bit older and wiser than me asked if I had got anywhere with her and when I told them they just laughed. I just kept repeating to them "I got the tit. I got the tit" and no matter what they said I was happy. Tommy, one of the lads who was older than me, said, "Charlie it's when you shag them that it's the real thing!" I said "What?" and he replied again "Its when you've had a shag that you know what its all about". I went home happy thinking about Joan Yates and what Tommy had said. A few weeks later on Joan Yates became the local fuck and got a right reputation for herself. What happened then was that my mates Sunny Clark, John Pollock and me would meet her after school and she would take us to the woods by Stockbridge Lane where she would lie on her back and pull her knickers to one side. The three of us would take it in turns to get on top of her and try our best to shag her, but we all couldn't seem to get it in and didn't have a clue what to do. We would all count to fifty before swapping over to ensure everyone had the same time with Joan. As I was stronger than Sunny and John though and they were a bit scared of me I got longer with Joan with them. When it was their turn I would count fast 1, 2, 3, 4, 5, 6, but when it was my turn I would tell the two of them they were counting too fast and slow them down 1...2...3...4...5...6... This was my first encounter with a girl, and later on in life when I got a lot of experience and became an expert at it, I would look back and laugh at my young foolish ways.

By now I was getting a reputation and a name for myself as being a bit wild "Don't go near that Charlie Seiga he split a kids head open with a slate and he's a bit crazy." I used this reputation to its utmost and started getting free passages over the Alt without my mates, my brothers or me being touched. As time passed and we all got a bit older we became pals with the Bootleites. Instead of shouting abuse the shouts became more friendly, "Hey your in our class aren't you?" "I know you don't I?" "Your kid's in our class isn't he?" It got to point where we were young teenagers who all knew about violence. They had been brought up living on the docks and seen some dreadful things because of the war. A lot of the kids stuttered from the atrocities they had seen. Today soldiers coming back from war overseas are given counselling and there is a new illness called "Post Traumatic Stress Disorder" which was first diagnosed after the Gulf War. These kids just got on with it but were clearly affected by what they had seen and were suffering. These Bootleite kids were the hardest kids I have ever come across. Even today I have a lot of friends who were born in Bootle and a lot of them are very hard men indeed.

Years later some of these hard Bootleite kids like jimmy Beattie and Tommy Stenson (Steno) became my staunch friends. They became notorious armed robbers and in the 1960's I did time in jail with some of them and became even closer friends. They were true criminals and hard as nails, never complaining at the punishment they received. Even if they got ten years bird they just got on with it and did it. That was what they were like even if the sentence was unfair. There was a large family called the Porters and Stevie Porter who was the main man in the family used to work on the docks. He was arrested for stealing two packs of kidneys off the docks but since he had a bit of a record and they couldn't nick him for anything else they did him for two packets of frozen kidneys that somebody else had actually given him. He went to the crown court and Justice Laskey, who by the way was a right bastard, gave him twelve years for the value of just a few pounds. I saw him years later and he was a broken man who looked old and tired. I don't know how the law society justifies such punishment only to say that they value money more than life.

I remember the first time I ever met Steno and Jimmy in 1963 when I had just been sent down for three years in Walton jail for being in possession of a shotgun and holding a bizzie at bay with it. The two men took me under their wing knowing I was a little bit down having been married just three weeks earlier, as well as them being mates with my older brothers. The three of us shared a cell for a long time, there was either one man to a cell or three in those days to try and stop any homosexual activity that may happen in a two-man cell. The two of them were serving quite a lengthy sentence for a large armed robbery they had been involved in down Bootle way. Steno had been brutally beaten up because the police who couldn't get a statement from him were bastards and had given him a going over with their batons and boots breaking his arms and ribs leaving him in a terrible mess. This was what happened then if you didn't co-operate with them, there were no taped interviews and solicitors present it was just their word against yours. The usual story would be that you had resisted arrest or attacked them; of course their word was always taken over yours. When we were in our cell Steno had told us all about what had happened to him and how bad the beating was.

All three of us got jobs in the prison reception wing, looking after incoming inmates, ensuring they were showered and had the right clothes to wear. Directing them where to go, what wing they were on and making sure they knew what was going on. I remember the day that Steno, a very hard man indeed who knew how to fight, telling us that the copper who had just arrived in the foyer with a handcuffed prisoner was one of the bizzies who had beat him. He went white and stood staring at the copper who had jumped him in his police cell a year earlier, not to mention told lies about him in court. Steno had a terrible temper on him and when the copper had the audacity to smile at Steno and take the piss by saying "Hello Tommy, how are you getting on with your bird? Is it dragging? Is it going slow for you?" he was hard to hold back as he just exploded with rage. The copper had to wait in a small room next to us, ready to go through to the final room in order to be released out of the prison. Steno went into the room where the copper was while we kept a look out. Steno went to town on him good style. He was dead fast punching fuck out of him and in no time at all the bizzie was in a terrible state and he was completely done in. Steno wasn't stupid though and he was quick thinking. He knew that if he was caught working a bizzie over he would be facing maybe five to seven years or more on top of his sentence. So before he went into the room where the bizzie was, he had ballied up (balaclava) with some bag he had copped for from the reception area. He knew he couldn't be identified. After he had finished working him over he went and got cleaned up straight away, getting shut of any incriminating evidence. He did get a good grilling over it, but he stuck to his story denying everything and nobody could prove a thing, especially the screws that had found the bizzie. We were all made up for him, that twat of a bizzie got what he deserved.

They were too sound fellas though and looked after me in the cell. The prison food in the late 1950s and early 1960's was diabolical and I remember the porridge we had to eat was made from pig meal where even the sack stated on it, 'grade A pig meal fit for human consumption'. We never saw an egg or a piece of steak like they do nowadays in their holiday camp prisons. Steno had a knack of catching pigeons for us to eat in our cell. He loved his food and he used to cook the pigeons on his homemade stove. The stove was a big old tin can that he had converted to be a small slow burning paraffin cooker. What he used to do was get a couple of carrots smuggled up from the prison kitchen and maybe an onion or two and set about laying a trap to catch a pigeon outside the small cell window. The window wasn't big enough to put your head out of but was certainly big enough for a bird to come in through! What he did was put some crumbs for the pigeon on the windowsill and catch them in his homemade trap. Sometimes he would even catch two. He would then set about plucking them, cleaning them and washing them ready for his night time pot.

When the lights went out at ten pm and all the screws had gone home, except the single guard left who usually spent his time down on the centre well away from the landings, Steno would get down to his cooking. The screws never came round to see what was going on, except every now and then when you would get a bastard spying on you through the spy hole in the door. Being a young kid I would soon drop off to sleep lying in my top bunk once the lights were out, but he always woke me up about two in the morning "Charlie, come on kid, get up." He had a pan of soup and a lovely cooked piece of pigeon for us all, sometimes he had even thrown some rice in to the gorgeous stock. We enjoyed his cooking and it got to the point that you could smell his beautiful, savoury, chicken like, cooking all over the landing. When the screws came in to work in the morning they would comment to us "Steno been at his cooking again?" well what could they do as it certainly wasn't coming from the kitchens which were well below us in the cellars of the prison.

One day Steno got called out of the cell on a visit and Beattie started to tell me about Steno and the pigeon lark. Beattie and Steno had been together since they were kids and times had been hard on the outside of jail too. Steno had learnt to cook the pigeons some years earlier when he was going through hard times with kids to feed. He lived in a flat in one of the tenement blocks just off the docks in Bootle. All the pigeons ate all the best food coming on and off the ships and were better than chickens. "Don't you think it's a bit bad eating the pigeons though?" I said, "They're not the best food in the world are they?" He stopped me and said "Listen kid, they eat the corn and peanuts from the docks and are lovely fat tasty birds." Steno used to have big opening windows in his flat and left food for the pigeons on the outside window ledge encouraging them into the flat with more food on the inside window ledge. He would sit and wait with a stick holding the window up ready for him to spring the trap when a couple of pigeons came in to feed. The window would slam down behind them once he gave that sticks string a tug and he would then catch and murder the pigeons in his room. He would sit for hours catching the poor birds ready for his pot.

Jimmy told me that he and his own family used to eat the pigeons too, and he said that he wanted the birds Steno caught for him to be kept alive so that they were fresh when he got them. There was no refrigerator to keep them fresh so a live bird would keep longer! One day Steno went round to Jimmy's flat with some pigeons ~ we used to call them micks~ for him freshly caught that morning. Jimmy said he could remember the birds well as there were two large common blue checks along with a little white much younger bird and Steno saying "These should do you Jimmy!" Once Steno left Jimmy's flat the two big birds were killed and prepared but the little squeaker didn't have enough meat on it and he couldn't kill it so he let it go and got on with the meal he was making with the other two birds. Two hours later Steno, who could be a bit moody at times and go into sulks if you fell out with him, knocked on the door. He opened the door with a cheerful smile only to be greeted by a right narky Steno saying "Hey Jimmy what the fucks going on?" "What do you mean like" replied Jimmy. Steno pulled the little white squeaker out of his jacket and thrust it at him "What are you playing at, I spend hours catching these fuckin' micks and you're just letting them go again! Well you get no fuckin' more off me in the future! I've just caught this one AGAIN, aren't my micks good enough for you?" with this he walked away with a cob on and wouldn't listen to his explanation of how scrawny that particular bird was. That was Steno with his moods, but besides all that the man was a good human being.

ENOUGH'S ENOUGH

Enough is enough as the saying goes. Well this was certainly true with our family, as my mother had had enough of life in and around our neighbourhood. She decided to move us through a house exchange to a different area in Huyton. Our Billy had just passed his eleven plus and was accepted to Prescot grammar school which we were all very proud about, I had just been expelled from my school for constant sagging so was moved to another secondary modern school called Finch Hall. She thought it would be a new start for us all, what with two of us moving schools anyway and our new neighbours not knowing our family history. My mother also thought that a change in environment would change my ways and bring out the best in me instead of the worst. When we moved to our new house this proved to be the worst thing she could have done for me, or was it? This is where I learnt my trade to be a villain and from here became one of Liverpool's high profile villains. The school didn't look down their noses at us, and the kids there were good friends to us. I still have a school photograph of my class and you can see just how poor all us kids were at that time. Times weren't too bad for us now, as the kids I was knocking about with knew what a bit of trouble was and what it was like to get in a bit of bother here and there. I think a lot of them had done a bit of pilfering as well because it opened my eyes as to how this other side of the neighbourhood was living. Life started to get exciting for me and I was all for it. Already rebelling and always accused of being a thief I thought I might as well be one, and get the rewards of my existing but undeserving reputation.

The best thing about me joining them and learning from them was that I became better than the lot of them. When I first started though there was routine we called the shopping bag caper that we all used to do. All the kids used to have big leatherette bags with long handles. The kids had to go into the shops shopping for their parents, there were no supermarkets to do a one-stop shop, and every shop had its own specialty, butcher, baker or even candlestick maker. The butchers only sold meat; no eggs or anything else and the veg shop didn't sell anything other than fruit and veg. This meant that there were shops that specialised in everything including sweets. The shopping bag caper was brilliant and I will never forget being shown how to do it for the first time. All the counters were quite high up coming up to kids chins and in the sweet shop there would be big jars of sweets on top of this counter, nougat bars, pear drops, barley sugars and various kinds of appetising sweets. There was a big demand for sweets as the war had ended and all sweet luxuries were well sought after having been missing for so many years. The two kids would walk into the sweet shop with one of these bags holding a handle each. When the woman or fella behind the counter a whole jar would be swept off the counter and plopped into the bag. It was that quick and clever the caper was brilliant. You could only ever get one in the bag as there was a chance of them breaking on top of each other and besides why get greedy and fuck everything up?

When it was my turn to do the caper we went to a sweet shop on Dinas lane in Page Moss. The shop had been nicknamed 'Tattyheads' after the woman who ran the shop, and the boys had already had a few jars from Tattyhead in the past. My mates thought she was starting to get on to us, but she still hadn't taken any precautions to stop us so we thought it would be ok. Most shops had a bell fitted on their front door that would ring whenever somebody entered the shop, this would help the owners run the shop when it was quiet. The owners would typically live in the back part of the shop and Tattyhead was no different living in the back of her shop. She didn't have a bell though and this was why my mates said she was getting hammered. I had never been in the shop before so didn't know the layout, but as me and Yank my mate who was holding the other handle of our bag pushed the door we heard Tattyheads new door bell ring. We thought eye-eye she must have started getting wise to what was going on but we went in anyway. We stood with our noses pressed up against that glass looking at the sweets ready to spend the couple of pennies we had ready to buy some sweets and not draw attention to ourselves. Tattyhead came out of the back room and looked like something out of the roaring twenties. She had bright red smudged lips and big round red cheeks painted with what must have been a gallon of rouge. She had a big woollen shawl wrapped around her shoulders and a funny smell of the olden days that I just couldn't pinpoint the origin of accompanied her into the room. She looked like Judy out of Punch and Judy and she had that type of scary face. Punch and Judy was meant to be funny but their distorted pointed faces always scared me.

Yank was determined to show me how it was done and have

something away from there, even if it was the last time we could hit her shop. We had been giving her the chat - "How much are those missus...What about those over there?" - all the time trying to get her to turn her back on us long enough for us to get one of the jars into our bag. When the opportunity arose Yank whispered "Now!" and I slid the big jar off the shelf towards our waiting bag. In my haste the jar overshot the bag we were holding and hit the floor. All hell let loose and Tattyhead came round the counter brandishing a big folded umbrella. "It was you bastards all the time robbing my sweets.... you bastards come back." We legged it out of the shop and down the street laughing our heads off all the way. That shopping bag job worked a treat and later on I made a good living out of it selling our goods to the kids on the fair. I became a little businessman knowing how to do things and sell things. It got to the point where the other kids were coming to me asking how to get shut of their gear or asking how much things were worth.

Some of the families in and around our new home in St David's Road had kids that I now became mates with, a new breed of Huyton kid I knew little about. At the end of our road was the old St David's church, now closed down and being used as a community hall. It had a big flat roof with balconies where we used to meet and all the little gangs hung around there and used it as their own social centre. Times were changing rapidly and the local kids started to cotton on to me more and more. Different families I was introduced to like the Doyle's who lived round the corner there was always a big pan of scouse or pea soup on the stove just simmering away. Their Mam, May Doyle, was a warm and friendly woman. She knew all about my background and what had happened to me and my family, but it didn't seem to matter to her and she treated me like one of her own sons Tommy and Joey (Joey was my best mate at the time). I would sometimes even stay overnight at the Doyle's and kip on their couch in front of the coal fire with an old blanket thrown over me. It reminded me of how our own house had been, warm, friendly and dead clannish. They still helped one another out borrowing goods from time to time. Other families that became close to me were the Myers, Anagans, Murphys and Fagains who were all of Irish decent and staunch Catholics. These people took to me instantly and welcomed me in with open arms. When you went into their houses you didn't feel intimidated or pulled down and I wanted to be with these people for the rest of my life.

What I didn't realise was that some of them were the best robbers I have ever seen in my life. I remember them showing me the neighbourhood where I used to play when I was younger and opening my eyes to what was really there. In the winter they all had 'winter warmers' which were empty baby milk cans that measured ten inches high by 7 inches wide. There were lots around as the estates were like breading grounds after the war and every house seemed to have a baby next to the fire drinking out of a bottle. They would add a piece of coat hanger wire to the tins to make a handle and pierce holes in the bottom and sides. These warmers were then set alight and could be swung about like a large Catherine-Wheel lighting up a winter's night. Some kids would even put a potato in them and we would all take a bite once it was cooked. The main function was to stand round them to keep warm. I had never seen anything like it before and to me it was all just brilliant.

Another popular game to play amongst my mates and me was Batman and Robin. All you could see on the estates was kids running about with raincoats (typically macs) tied round their necks to form a cape and the rest of the coat spread open and trailing behind in the wind. Everyone wanted to be a hero and Batman or Robin seemed to be the ones that most kids favoured. But me being me, I wanted to be different from the rest of the crowd, so one day while my mates, me and my brothers played in our back garden, I robbed a large piece of rolled up black cloth that I hastily cut into a cloak. I even made slits in the cloak where my hands and arms would slot through to make real wings and leave my hands free for all sorts of silly capers ~ most kids just held on to their coat tails that flew behind them to give their wings some structure. When I made my real wings and having a very active imagination, I totally believed I could fly. I made a big impression in our back yard to my mates showing off my new cape and wings. Of course none of my mates or brothers would believe I could fly no matter how hard I tried to convince them. There was nothing for it except to prove it once and for all, I knew I only had to keep a tight hold of the wings to ensure the holes my arms went through wouldn't rip and flying would be easy. So I started to climb the drainpipe up our back wall making my way to the roof. I was a good climber and found this dead easy, even though my brothers were shouting at me to forget it all and come back down before I got killed. When I finally reached the slate roof, I stood upright with both my feet at the edge of the cast iron gutters. I looked down at my mates below and I seemed to be right up in the sky, my brothers were still shouting and our Jimmy put his hands over his eyes and shouted "Charlie, no kid don't do it, don't do it!" All the kids below now started chanting

"ONE...TWO...THREE..." and on that I looked down and thought to myself 'I know I can do this and I know for a fact I can fly.' As I threw myself off the roof the chanting stopped and the back yard became quiet as I plummeted towards the ground. I tried to glide but I was just tumbling like a brick. I hit my Ma's clothesline that stretched right across the back yard, which luckily broke my fall instead of my neck, before snapping, and landing me with a crash on the floor. I came out of it okay; just suffering some bumps and bruises. That was my first and last flying experience and at the same time I fuckin' sacked that Batman and Robin lark off moving on to new adventures.

THE DABS

The Dabs was a nickname for Lord Derby's estate and mansion set in huge grounds on the outskirts of Liverpool. It was surrounded by a huge seven-foot wall, which we used to get a 'leg up and over' to go robbing apples and to fuck about. As soon as we got over the wall we were in a different country, it was dead exciting full of meadows and rhododendron trees. They had lots of game and we would often see deer and pheasants along with rabbits and other smaller wildlife. There was a danger though, I had been told at all times to watch for the gamekeeper. He had a big shotgun and wouldn't think twice about shooting you thinking you would be a poacher. He was a vicious and nasty bastard that we were all scared to death of. This day when Owen Murphy (the cock of our gang) asked me to go over the Dabs and make our way to 'White Mans Dam' I was made up to go. We had to crawl across meadows and fight our way through the thick thickets of the woodland to get there, it was real un-chartered territory and there was no tree thinning or cut backs, it was all growing wild. The name itself 'White Mans Dam' gave me a buzz and drove me on regardless of any danger. We thought we were just like Robin Hood in that woodland. Every now and then the cry "Everybody down" would be given as a gamekeeper or horse and rider were spotted on the long road to the mansion. It wasn't far now I was told and soon we emerged into the last meadow before the luring 'White Mans Dam' and I was totally psyched up. If we had made it to 'White Mans Dam' I knew I would be one of the cocks of the gang and would have gained a lot of respect. Owen Murphy who had a big mop of red hair said, "Here it is now Charlie." As I came out of the bushes I couldn't believe my eyes, we were on the edge of a lake that was shimmering in the sun. There were huge dragonflies skipping on the water and I was amazed at its spectacle. I was quickly told never to swim in the lake as the pike were big, massive things like sharks that would drag you under, they were even known to have pulled fully grown swans to their deaths in the depths below.

Just beyond the lake was a huge white mansion with large Georgian windows reaching down to the ground. Every now and then you could just make out some movement in the windows and we would all duck down and be quiet. Little did I know that years later I would be screwing these types of mansions and having the silver, jewellery and antiques away from them. In the early 1950's two footmen at the mansion had a dual to the death over Lady Derby ~they were both giving her one! They ended up shooting each other dead and are buried to this day in a small field just outside the lord's estate not being allowed a churchyard burial near the aristocracy. Typical of all the English blue bloods they always try to cover up any real scandals about themselves, don't they? I used to rob from those rich bastards and I'm not one bit ashamed of it, after all how did they become rich in the first place? Years later I read a confidential police memo that had fallen into my hands, I can't say how, where or when. It does quote one copper that says 'The amount of antiques that were stolen by Liverpool villains in the early 1970's was so big that the regional crime squad set up a separate antiques squad looking into these thefts that were allegedly controlled by Charlie Seiga. He was their number one target for all these high class antique robberies.' ~ As an aside, I would just like to take this opportunity to show my sincere gratitude to all those rich lords and ladies who made my life a bit more comfortable – 'thank you very much indeed for your generosity!'

We were nearly back to the wall by now and so far so good, when all of a sudden the gamekeeper spotted us and he came running like fuck after us. It was the evil bastard we all knew about and who we called Bandy Legs due to his oddly shaped bowlegs. Everybody gave the shout "Watch out its Bandy Legs is coming." "Quick Bandy Legs has got a gun, get to the wall." Everybody scattered and without any hesitation at all he let his gun go off. I lost my bottle altogether at all the screams and I quickly hid myself in leaves behind a big bush. I then saw Bandy Legs come past in his big buckled boots, shouting and yelling. I saw his face and it looked really evil and scared me especially with his long crinkly hat. I could hear the twigs breaking as he ran and I heard the gun go off again. I stayed there until dusk waiting for it to be really safe before making my way back to the wall and away home safe and sound.

When I was a lot older about 18, my mates and me decided to go over the Dabs just for a laugh and re-enact our trip to the dam. Once over the wall we were transformed back into our childhood again, even whispering and creeping about nice and low to ensure we weren't seen. We had got a long way in before Bandy Legs saw us again and started to give chase. We ran towards the safety of the wall again just like when we were kids and he even tried to cut us off down a little pathway. Eventually he let his gun go at us with a shout of anger. I didn't like this at all and stopped my mates from running saying we were grown men now, and that why should we be scared of this twat of a gamekeeper, after all we had done fuck all wrong. So we turned to face him with me in the middle waiting for him to emerge from his thrashing through the trees. As he did and saw us waiting his run turned to a jog and then to a walk before eventually stopping dead in his tracks about five yards in front of me. It was my turn now, so I walked over to him dead slow. When I got there I had the shock of my life, he was only small and I could see he was well past it, not like myself, I had just got out of borstal and was a fit young man. He said "What are you doing over here? You know your trespassing!" You could smell him a mile away, and when he spoke I could see his rotten teeth. I wouldn't like to get a bite off him, not with those black teeth he would most probably poison you. I said "Don't you remember me? I was a little kid you terrorised for years when we weren't doing anything wrong." "Well it's my job to keep you off Lord Derby's land and I was just doing my job." He retorted. "I know who you are you little fucker" I said " I'm going to take that gun of yours and ram it up your arse. You little bastard!" With this I kicked him up the arse and we started chasing him with cries of "Get him. Get the dirty little fucker" until he was out of sight over the meadows, we were all laughing our heads off that much we just couldn't run anymore. That was the last time I ever saw Bandy Legs!

During those years in the summer holidays my brothers and me were sent to New Brighton to get out of my Ma's way. It wasn't only my brothers and me; most kids at that time were forced to go there during the summer. In order to get to New Brighton we needed to take a tram ride and then catch the so-called famous ferry across the Mersey. Today there is a pleasant stigma attached to all things Liverpool like the ferry and the Beatles. Most of the people who bring up the old Liverpool nostalgia locally are not even true Scousers. I'm not saying all, but some of the people working on local newspapers, the council and the radio are mostly wooly backs and out of towners from other parts of the country and they don't really understand the background of these scouse celebrities. The Beatles were of course a worldwide phenomenon and brought a lot of good fortune to Liverpool as well as some great music. There were many other local bands that played much better music but never got the recognition that the Beatles did. The Cavern club is known worldwide as the birthplace of the Beatles, which every true Scouser knows is just not true. The Beatles played all over Liverpool in many clubs and pubs and the Cavern is just one example of where their roots came from. When people talk about the ferry, it seems that it is a boat of pleasure and in recent times has become a focus for British sightseers and foreign tourists alike. Gerry and the Pacemakers, in their legendary song 'Ferry Cross The Mersey', of course brought it to notoriety. The image of romantic days when you and your girl would have pleasant boat trips isn't how I recall the ferry, indeed I have a very different recollection of the ferry from my summer childhood days. I fuckin' dreaded it. So as regards to the magical 'Ferry Cross the Mersey', to us kids it was just one big headache as we were lucky to get a spec on the crowded New Brighton smelly beach. As far as these outsiders, who are not true scousers but wrote all of those so-called nice stories about Liverpool life, they just didn't know the reality of what went on. As far as Gerry who goes on to state 'and here I'll stay' as one of the lyrics in his popular song, well it's just a load of bollocks as he fucked off out of Liverpool when he made a few quid. So too did the Beatles and Cilla Black who voted Tory and became a Conservative ~by the way these scouse celebs were all supposed to be working class people, working class my arse.

The six-week school holiday, like today, was a real nuisance to my parents even back then. It meant that us kids would be under my Ma's feet all day hanging about the house and getting into all sorts of trouble that we really shouldn't be. We used to have to try and keep ourselves amused but on many days we were told to get ourselves out of the area and spend the day on the beach at New Brighton. A trip to the beach today may be many kids dream day out, but back then it involved a tedious journey and grim day with no money to enjoy the fun of the seaside. Like many of my mates we would be told of our immanent day out and knew what was to happen. The day started with my Ma making us the traditional doorstop jam butties and wrapping them for us in an old newspaper tied up with a piece of string. There would be a package for me, and one each for my three younger brothers too. For a drink my Ma would have collected four empty milk bottles. Unlike today where you hardly see a milk bottle and most people get their milk from a supermarket in a plastic carton every household had their milk delivered by the local milkman and it came in many different ways. There was the regular silver top bottle, which is the same as full fat today, there was also a more expensive gold top, which had a far thicker creamy consistency to it. The standard milk most people drank was the thinner 'stery' or sterilized milk, which came in a longer thinner bottle that had a very long neck, much like a wine bottle of today. It was these bottles that my Ma needed for our day trip. She had already been to the shop and bought some lemonade powder, which was a yellowish powder that you added to tap water and then shook as hard as you could to dissolve the powder. It never really dissolved properly and the sediment could always be seen at the bottom of the bottle. The bottle would need to be corked with rolled up old newspapers to stop the liquid from escaping, which inevitably it always did.

Once ready we were sent on our way. There used to be penny return tickets on the trams where as a kid you would get a trip to Liverpool and back for a penny. The tram conductor would tear your ticket in half on the outward journey and you would give the other half in to get home at the end of the day. After our tram ride from Huyton to the Pier Head we then had to catch the ferry from the landing stage opposite the Liver Buildings to New Brighton. The Mersey itself is today and always has been, a murky black, smelly river. By the time we arrived at New Brighton we had been travelling for an hour or more and we were knackered. Most of the drink from our bottles had been spilt or leaked along the way and we would head straight to the beach already starving. When we would open our parcels of butties there would always be sand in them and we just couldn't eat them. No matter how hard you tried, or how perfectly you wrapped those butties up the sand always got into them. That sand made the sandwiches taste like we were just chewing grit. It was horrible! We would end up famished with no money to go on the fairgrounds and be totally miserable all day. We would end up just walking round looking at the things we would like to do or buy but just didn't have the money for. We did a lot of wishful thinking.

The misery and hunger of those days to New Brighton drove me to start on the other lark (stealing). I would wonder into the shops on the promenade and would steal anything I could see. Any food I saw lying about would be easy pickings for me and I would have it away. Apples, biscuits, a couple of cakes from a tray, or anything else would soon be targeted for my brothers and me to help fill our bellies. This was all before facing our gruelling return journey home. If you lost your tram or bus ticket you would be in real trouble and some of the conductors could be right bastards and not let you on. As it was a good few miles home this would put a real dampener on your day. Sometimes if you had the bottle you would leg the tram. When the tram started moving you would jump on the back and hang on to the big steel rails, clinging on for your life. If you got a real bastard conductor he would let rip at you as you hung on trying to smash you with the big leather belt that he used to hang his money bag over his shoulder. He wouldn't half give you a pounding until you fell off. Most kids would be screaming for him to stop the tram so you could get off safely but he never would, he would just continue with his ruthless whipping. ~ These overhead cable trams have long gone from Liverpool but they are now thinking of re-introducing them to ease the growing traffic congestion. These hard New Brighton trips were a nightmare for us all and we hated them. When we were older though, with money in our pockets the trips would be fun as we could spend on the fairs and do all the things we wished we could do years earlier.

We used to get up to all kinds of other mischief in the summer holidays too. One favourite one was to go legging lorries down the dock road. We were always down the dock road as this place always had an attraction to us with lots going on with a bit of this and a bit of that. Kids from all over Liverpool used to congregate on the dock roads looking for peanuts. Peanuts were big business back then and a big factory called Bibbys used to be a main target. They used to haul the peanuts in 'Puffing Billys', which were steam driven motor wagons with a small fire in the cab keeping the engine going. The old ashes from the furnace would drop into a big pan suspended under the cab and you could see the red-hot ash blowing away on windy days. These Billys couldn't go as fast as a normal petrol wagon and so were easier for kids to skip or jump on the back of. All the sacks would be stacked up neatly and it would be easy to see what they were carrying. We used the jagged cut lids of tin cans that we had foraged for in local bins, as knives to slice open the sacks and reveal their contents. We would then fill our pockets, jumpers and anything else we could carry with the gushing peanuts that poured from the sliced sacks, before jumping off and filling our faces. Other Billys carried 'sticky-lishe' which were short twigs that you chewed to get the sweet taste from before they swelled up too much to eat. We used to think we were like cowboys with that sticky-lishe as the stuff reminded us of how cowboys chewed tobacco before spitting it out in a brown mess. They were horrible really but as a kid seemed a real treat. Some Billys carried brown sugar and the same procedure would happen to those, with kids slicing open the sacks, the main difference here though was that the sugar was easier to sell later on. Robbing peanuts off the backs of Billys was a regular thing for us but once I got caught by a couple of old Dockers. They grabbed me by the scruff of my neck giving me a terrible fright. They asked if I realised where the sacks had been or how they were stored, which of course I hadn't a got a clue about. They told me that the peanuts were stored in warehouses full of rats and at night time the rats would run on the sacks and piss on the peanuts. They told me I would be lucky not to be poisoned by them ending with the customary "Get back home you little bugger!" with a good clip around the ear. There was nothing I could do though as it was customary for adults to smack children, not like today where kids can report their parents for a smack across the head. Teachers are scared of the consequences today; if a kid doesn't have a go itself its parents will come round and have a go at you instead. The cane never did me or my mates any harm and we grew up better behaved and more respectful for it, there's just no discipline left for kids in society anymore.

Saturday mornings were the best for me and it was dead exciting as you would see huge gangs of kids making their way to St Johns Market in the city centre. At the back of the market there were all kinds of wonderful stalls selling a multitude of animals. There were pigeons in small cages, chickens, little puppies and kittens in cages along with fish galore. The caged animals were kept warm by the small flames from an array of gas fuelled Bunsen Burners. The market was fascinating to me, and a brilliant sight. As well as being an opportunity to do some slight pilfering from the more traditional stalls. You would see the other kids there too and it soon became apparent that the kids from Scottie road were the widest of us all. They would pull boxes pilled high with wood they took and other goodies from the fish and fruit markets along the streets back towards Scottie road on steery carts or old prams. The Scottie road kids would always be fighting with us too. The cock of their gang and the cock of our gang would have a scrap to see who was the hardest and to win some pride and respect. The Scottie road gangs were dead wide and could sell anything at all. They knew all the tricks of the trade and their strong Catholic Irish upbringing made them strictly disciplined streetwise kids. They knew how to live on the streets and make money from whatever opportunity was put in front of them. They could out think most people and con their way into making a few quid. Some of these kids became my friends and in later years we ended up doing some armed robberies together and other villainous acts.

The council houses in the poorer areas had a thriving cottage industry of trades and that is where most of the wood that the Scottie road kids took ended up. It was broken down in to manageable chunks and sold as firewood door to door. Other kids had paper rounds to make money but I was getting bang into the easier way of making money. Sometimes we would sell the brown sugar or other goodies from the docks that we had robbed always aware that the bizzies would be looking for us. The bizzies were the street kids archenemies and we would always look out for one another and give a shout when we saw one coming. Some houses had their own way of making money just like Four Penny Jims the barber. The Kelly family who lived a few door away made toffee apples to sell to the kids, using the old green sour apples that had been robbed from a fruit and veg shop with a chopped up firewood stick rammed into it. The stick would be really rough and never smoothed down with a bit of sandpaper so you often got splinters from them. You had to be really careful when eating the apple close to the stick, as there is nothing more painful as a kid than getting a splinter in your mouth or gum and everybody having a go at trying to get it out for you. The toffee that covered the apples was made from the brown sugar they had bought from some kid who had thieved it from the back of a Billy at the docks the day before. Colin Woods's house on Wimbourne road used to sell chips from their back kitchen. There would be a big old frying pan full of dripping going and a line of kids queuing up to buy two penneth of the part cooked chips. They would be wrapped in an old piece of newspaper and thrust at the kid who would wolf them down not caring if they were not cooked properly as long as they were hot; it was the done thing to do. My mate Yank Myers and his family sold homemade ice cream off a cart. Yank had to peddle that fuckin' cart up and down the roads ringing a big brass bell selling his homemade ice cream.

Life was great for me, and my newfound community made me extremely welcome. I felt that I fitted in well to my new way of life and progressed quickly as I started to sag school almost every day to be with my new mates. I was starting to run wild and forming my own gang becoming streetwise and understanding the rules of living on the streets of Liverpool. The older men would be seen on street corners playing a game we kids called 'pigeon toss' ~ this form of gambling more commonly called toss was just throwing two penny coins up in the air for a game of heads or tails. I would sometimes act as lookout for these old fellas in case any bizzies came sniffing by to earn a few coppers, as street gambling was illegal in those days. I would stand on the corner of the street looking for a bizzie on a bike to appear and then give the shout "Watch out here come the bizzies" when the old fellas would scatter like fuck and the gambling would move to a different location. This was the same for the card schools. There were card schools everywhere and if all else failed they would play on the open fields always ready for a quick off-man. I was a good lookout and got a lot of work from these fellas and even started running bets for the bookies. All my mates had little jobs they did; we lived on our wits and made a life for ourselves on the streets. My new mates taught me how to do a lot of these jobs and between us we became good shoplifters, which turned into a good earner and really took off.

Like a lot of other kids I had a legitimate Saturday job in order to give me a few extra quid. As a growing lad I was hungry all the time, getting a mans appetite and always had a roaring appetite so a part time job at Peagrams the local grocers store in Page Moss and Dovecote suited me well. I was only stacking shelves, sweeping up and other minor jobs but it gave me some great opportunities. Early on a Saturday morning I had to bring out the produce from the back storeroom and take it to the front shop to fill the shelves. While doing this I had access to all sorts of goodies which I eagerly took advantage of. There were numerous tins of fruit in the storeroom, peaches, pears and pineapples all of which were seen as luxuries. Now I knew I couldn't rob them, as they were counted quite regularly, but I had a better way of making the best of the situation. I always carried a small pocket pen knife, much like a Swiss army knife with me and I used this to help pull back the seam of the label on the cans just far enough so that I could see the tin itself below. I would then switch the blade of my knife to be a sharp point and would pierce the can with a quick hard blow. The juice could then easily be poured out into an old cup and I would drink it fast without anybody seeing before putting the label back over the hole and replacing the tin back on the shelf without even leaving a trace. This went on for a few weeks and the customers started coming into the shop complaining that there was no juice in their luxury fruit cans. "There's not as much juice in these cans as there used to be, is there?" they would ask, never knowing where it had all gone. I was never caught doing that and nobody ever sussed on about it.

The end of the job did come though when I was caught red handed. It was the end of my shift and almost knocking off time, I had got a few items stashed down my jumper that I had accumulated during the day in my secret store. I had the items secured by means of my snake s-clasp belt that held my jumper tight and I had a bomber jacket zipped up over the top. I didn't have loads down my jumper but I did have enough. My stolen shopping included a couple of wagon wheels, a block of best butter, a few slices of rolled up ham that I fancied and various other little items. Just as I was leaving the shop with my stash down my jumper the efficient owner, Mr. Butler who always wore a long brown overall with pockets full of pens and papers, called my name out and I stopped dead in my tracks thinking he has sussed me out here and I'm caught bang to rights. He was a real firms man and liked to stand behind the bacon counter ensuring it wasn't cut too thick and the most profit was made from each side of bacon. "Can you do me a favour before you go home Charlie?" "Certainly yes" I replied with a sigh of relief that I hadn't been sussed out. He asked me to go up a ladder and pass him some packets of dried currants and raisins down to him. They were on a high shelf wrapped in dark blue packets with a sticky label over them and I knew I might come unstuck here. I got the stepladder and went up hesitantly. At the top I still couldn't reach the currants easily and had to stretch a bit leaning over to get the bags. As I passed the first bag down to him my belt burst open and a block of best butter hit Mr. Butler right on his fuckin' head. He was shocked and didn't know what had hit him, the next minute the rest of my stash fell on top of him as well. "Come down Charlie" he said in a slow quiet voice, taking me into the back room. He was very disappointed in me, as he knew my troubled background before giving me the job and had given me a good chance. I had broken his trust and he asked me to leave and never go back. I couldn't wait to get out of that shop door minus all my goodies but to give him some credit he never called the bizzies, which he could easily have done. I should probably have thanked him for that.

Seasonal jobs were good earners for kids too. The season I went spud picking was a turning point in my young life and is when I got into the burglary game. The farmers used to pick up a group of us young workers on his tractor pulling a big cart and take us off miles and miles into the countryside to help him pick his crops. We were being used as child labour, everybody knew but since it was our choice to sag off school, ~ even parents would sometimes keep their kids off school especially to go spud picking and bring in some extra cash ~ and the farmer needed to get his crop picked cheaply nobody said a word. The farmers knew we needed the money and worked us hard, they were bastards to us city kids working us hard until we thought our backs would break. One day I was late and missed the farmer's cart having to walk all the way out to the farm on my own. When I got there I was about an hour late and the farmer was livid. "Your late.... Get your arse onto the field and get picking with the rest of them, you lazy little sod!" He used to give each worker a length of field to work marked out by two sticks, usually about ten yards. This was the area you had to cover in the day in order to get paid. Well he gave me an enormous length of around twelve yards because I was late and wanted to get a bit more work out of me. Well my heart sagged and this made my mind up that this life just wasn't for me. At the end of the day when it was getting dark we would knock off and queue up outside the stable door. The farm was owned by two brothers called the Butch-Yards, and old Joe Butch-Yard was a real nasty bastard who had made my days there hell. He used to haunch over the stable door and play with the money in his hands teasing the queuing workers all eager to get their pay out. Everyone used to get four bob a day in the form of two silver shilling pieces from old Joe before heading back up the dirt track to the waiting cart ready for the long journey home. On this occasion he made me wait at the back of the queue to get my money and told me that he was only going to pay me half the days wages for being late and would dock me one whole shilling. This did my head in and my temper started getting the better of me, not only had I worked hard to catch up with the others I had also done a bigger length, but being a kid what the fuck could I do. When the queue eventually went and it was my turn to be paid he had run out of money. He told me to hang about while he went and fetched me the shilling he was going to pay me. As the bastard headed off to the farmhouse door my mates started dawdling up the lane without me heading for the cart. I could see him enter the house and turn the lights on. I wondered over to the house and he told me to wait by the front door. Standing by the door I could see through the front room window and peered in to see him walk over to a big grandfather clock in the corner of the room. The clock had a big door on it with a big brass keyhole drilled into it, but he just pulled the door open not even needing the key. He put his hand into the well of the grandfather clock and pulled out a bag. He put the bag on the table and opened it up taking out some money. All this time he had no idea that I was watching him through the window. He put the money in his pocket and put the bag back in the well of the grandfather clock before finally pushing the old door back into place. I quickly returned to the front door and waited for him. He came out and thrust the single shilling into my hand saying, "Next time don't be late otherwise your getting the sack!" He knew himself that we all needed the money and that I would have to come back to work the next day.

Once the cart had dropped us off I turned to my mate Joey Hannagan and told him that we wouldn't be going to pick spuds in the morning, I've got a cracking job for us its dead easy. I told him everything about the farmer's stash and where it was kept. Joey, who was a good shoplifter anyway, was dead game and we decided to get our own back on that evil slave driving bastard. The next day we didn't turn up to the cart pick up point, instead we set off on our bikes towards the farm. Our bikes were of course stolen; we would take the wheels off one bike and put them on the frame of another before painting it a different colour to disguise them. We arrived half an hour after the cart would have got there knowing the daily routine intimately. We knew the house would be empty with all the kids, the farmer and his wife out on the field working right up until the farmer's wife came back to make a big steel urn of tea to take back to the workers ready for dinner time when the kids would stop for ten minutes to eat their butties and have a drink from that urn. When we got to the farm itself we hid our bikes behind some bushes and peered over the low farm wall. We could see them all in the field in the distance working with the bastard, miser, farmer driving up and down hunched over the wheel of his tractor making sure the kids were working hard as usual. I remember that cold freezing October morning it was really bitter that day.

While they were busy working I said to Joey "Come on, let's get it done. I'll go in and get it; I know exactly where it is. You stay outside and keep a good lookout." I turned the big old brass door knob slowly, and I mean slowly as to not make a noise, even though I knew nobody could hear me and suddenly it just opened wide. Nobody locked their doors then as there was no need, everybody trusted each other and these sorts of robberies were very rare. It was warm inside as there was a big coal fire burning in the grate. I could hear the grandfather clock in the front room ticking, tick tock, tick tock, tick tock. The noise of the ticking seemed to grow louder and louder as I got closer and it made my heart pump faster and louder than ever before. Was I going to get caught? Was I going to get trapped? Would the clock fall on me and trap me so I was there when the farmers wife came home? I was so nervous as I had never been in a farmhouse before let alone do a robbery. I started to realise there were other clocks ticking in the house too and soon my whole head was swimming with the noise of clocks ticking. I thought I could feel eyes on me but it was just the clocks making me uneasy. I was dead scared in case something happened, and the fear of being in this house was really freaking me out. Even a cuckoo coming out from one of those clocks would have made me turn and run not looking back until I was well away from this terrifying place. Even at my slow creeping pace, ensuring I didn't make a sound, I eventually reached the grandfather clock. It was huge seeming to almost touch the ceiling. Its face was dull but over ornate, with weird markings engraved where the numbers should be and its big brass hands had a striking paisley design on them. The casing itself was well polished and stood there like a big dark guards century box. It was very intimidating and as I started to pull the door open I could feel my heart reach my mouth. I reached inside taking care not to touch the swinging pendulum and felt about. To my surprise there seemed to be not just one bag in there, but three. I pulled out the bags one at a time and placed them on the floor beside me. They were of a course material and reminded me of flour bags. When I opened the first heavy bag I could see it was full of coins just like the one I had seen farmer Joe with the night before ready to pay out the kids wages. The second bag was full of gold sovereigns and chains; I couldn't believe what I was seeing. If I thought that was treasure I was wrong because when I opened the third bag my eyes were popping out of my head. The bag was filled with big white five-pound notes! I grabbed the bags and left as quickly as I could, telling Joey who was still keeping lookout outside what I had found. We put the bags down our pullovers and peddled like fuck, getting away as fast as possible never to return.

The stash we got from that grandfather clock that day was too much for us kids to take in and we thought we were millionaires. We took the bags to our den to decide what to do with it all. The first thing we did was get some old tin cans and bury them all under the den. Our den was in the field behind our house, we had dug a big hole and put some corrugated iron over the top from a derelict bomb shelter and then covered the top with sods of grass to make it camouflaged. Our den was the safest place we knew at that time and we knew that it would be okay there. We needed to find a way of getting the cash in smaller chops easier for kids to spend. Joey said he knew a woman who would mind it for us and give us some as and when we needed it. So Joey introduced me to Winnie who lived at the end of our road. She was a big black haired woman and was a real Fagin. She knew all the tricks of the trade and would show kids how to steal for her. She was a real dirty bitch too and would sometimes tease us kids showing us her fanny asking us what we thought. That was the first real fanny I saw, a big black hairy monster that we would just stare at in awe. One of our mates, little Terry Burns, who was fascinated by her fanny used to egg Winnie on saying "Go on Winnie, lets see it again, go on show us." She used to tease little Terry whenever he asked to see more until one day when he was stood really close having a close examination of her black muff she gave him a closer look. She suddenly grabbed the back of his head and pulled his face to her, rubbing herself on him and waggling ferociously. It must have been sloppy and wet all over his little face as when she let her grip go he ran to the corner coughing and spluttering. We all stood watching open mouthed and in total silence. Little Terry never asked for a second look again and got himself right at the back of the crowd when Winnie did her flashing routines to us with her big stinking hairy mott.

Joey who was eighteen months older than me, a clever and wide lad, told me that we must just spend our money in bits here and there. He said his dad would get rid of the notes for us if we wanted but that Winnie was the one to help with the gold. Being a kid I didn't know how much our haul was worth but it must have been quite a few hundred pounds, which back then was a fortune. I told Joe I wanted to give some money to my Mam but without her knowing, leaving it about so she wouldn't know where it had come from. We can do that he said, but first we need to get Winnie to help us. Joey being streetwise knew not to show Winnie all our stash and so we gave it to her a bit at a time starting with some gold sovereigns and a bundle of five-pound notes, but even with this minor stash her eyes lit up when she saw what we had got. She asked where we had got it from and we told her. She then told us not to tell anybody else what we had, where we had got it or even that we had given some to her. "This is our secret lads, don't tell anybody as you know how rumours get spread around here, and the jealousy that will follow." We had already decided to play it down and keep a low profile.

The first thing we did with our new found wealth was to go on a mad spending spree. Fields surrounded all the council houses in those days and this is where the gypsies used to camp and pitch their travelling fairs. They had all sorts of rides and stalls, the waltzer, the scare ~ ghost train, the dodgems and much more. The gypsies never asked questions if a kid was on the fair spending money, you just had to be careful that you weren't caught with a big stash on you by the local bizzies.

I told Winnie that I wanted to give some money to my Ma and she started giving me coins and the odd ten bob note that I could slip into my Ma's purse without her knowing. This went on for five to six weeks with my Ma asking, "Where did this money come from?" Well there was only me and my brothers in the house so she knew it was me and she knew what I was becoming, but there was no way she could stop me. She would say, "Charlie is this yours?" I would just shrug and walk away. I was living the good life now, I had rebelled and nobody was going to change me.

Winnie creamed a lot of the dough off our stash and fucked us left right and centre but we still had enough to do what we wanted and as kids we thought we were doing well and were buzzing like fuck with all the money. If hadn't been for Joey she would have had us for a lot more than what she did. He would always pull her up when she was trying it on saying "Hang on a minute it wasn't three sovereigns we gave you yesterday it was five in my matchbox! Give us what you owe us Winnie!" ~ Joey always carried his coins in a matchbox stuffed inside with a bit of cotton wool you see, so he always knew what he had.

We lived like lords from then on and we raided a lot more farms. This was our big take as kids and we were earning a lot of money. What we used to do during the picking seasons was ride our bikes out to the different farms and ensure the farmers were in the fields with the workers before peering through the windows and entering the house and searching for their stash. It was always hidden in different places and I soon realised that I was lucky with my searching and had a nose for spotting where the cash was hidden. If we didn't find the readies we would always spin the place over and find gold and silver pocket watches, which although wasn't the jackpot certainly made our efforts worthwhile. I carried this talent on in later years while searching for safes in stately homes and offices. The farms were never locked up and it was always easy pickings. We used to give the door a bit of a knock first in case there was an old grandmother milling about inside. If the door was answered we used to say we were on a long bike ride and tired from all the peddling so could we have a glass of water please. They always obliged and we would just turn about and be on our way. Once we weren't too lucky, entering a farmhouse we believed was empty and creeping towards the lounge. The door to the lounge was a bit sticky and I had to use a bit of force with my shoulder to barge it open. Sat on the other side was an old woman deeply engrossed in her knitting sat in a big chair. She must have been stone deaf, as she never flinched. I quickly backed up and got out of that house as quickly as I could, as my bottle had totally gone by then, knowing that If we had been caught by the farmer he would have shot us dead, taking the law into his own hands. But can you blame him though?

Winnie must have had a good fence to get rid of the amount of stash we took back to her to dispose of on our behalf. It was because of our antics that eventually all the farmers started chaining big Alsatians to their doors to stop us getting in. The word of what we were up to must have spread round the farming community and at the end had to stop our little jobs. Funnily enough there never seemed to be any bizzies about, and it was years later when I found out that some of the farms I had robbed off were bang at it themselves too.

As a real active villain in my twenties, with my own team working with me, we would be bang into hijacking wagons and their containers full of copper, brass, bronze or even spirits or ciggies. We would force the driver out of his cab, tie him up and leave him somewhere to be found later on when we were well away. Some of the drivers were in on the jobs and knew what was about to happen. They would just go for a piss leaving us to take their wagon without any fuss at all. These farmers would offer us a safe place to store the trailers while we got a buyer. This went on for quite some time with everyone getting a cut at the weigh in (pay out). These places were called the 'slaughters' as this was where the goods were chopped up ready to be sold on and farmer's barns made great slaughterhouses. One day while we were at a slaughter we went in to talk to the farmer. Well I realised that I had been there before and that as a kid I had stolen a load of cash and pocket watches from this guy. I started to feel a bit guilty about what I had done, especially when the fella came up to me and shook my hand saying "Nice to see you Charlie." We sat around the farmhouse table all getting weighed in while his wife made a pot of tea and I was thinking to myself.... little do you know that years ago I robbed your takings and I bet you wouldn't be as pleasant with me now if you knew that... I felt sorry for what I had done to him as he seemed such a nice person, but I was a hungry little kid then and he had more than he could possibly need, but I couldn't tell him that now sat round his kitchen table, could I?

We never told anybody about those farmhouse robberies as kids that kept us well fed, clothed and in supply of American comics, and as Joey, god bless his sole, has since passed away this is the first time that the story has ever been revealed.

REAL STREETWISE

It had just turned 1954 and was slightly before my fourteenth birthday and at that age you starting to change into a young man and the appetite I had before was even stronger now. The year was still early and the weather was cold. I would be out till all hours with my mates and out of my Ma's control. After a Saturday night courting at a weekend I would often arrive home at 12pm or 1am in the morning, which in those days was dead, dead late. It was easier to stay out late on a Saturday night as Sunday mornings were traditionally a morning where you could lie in bed a lot longer than any other day of the week. I would come home, creeping down the back entry and enter the house via the back kitchen door; it would always be open as nobody locked their back doors then. I was always wary of my old man, and didn't want to wake him as we never got on and I was still a bit scared of him. What happened every Saturday was that all the women used to buy their weekend joint of meat. Most women would make a trip to St Johns market and wait until it was almost closing time before grabbing a bargain of a cheap piece of meat that the butchers couldn't keep until Monday. There were no fridges about and meat soon went bad. Most council houses just had a cold shelf inside their pantries and that was where you tried to keep your perishable goods cool. My Ma, like most women, would get a big piece of beef, lamb or pork for buttons this way but knew she had to cook it the same day, as it would probably start to go off. When I came home on a Saturday night the big tin roasting dish was always in the oven where the joint had been part cooked in a big lump of dripping. It would be waiting for Sunday morning when the oven would be re-lit and the joint cooked in full, this of course kept the meat from going bad.

When I came back home I would be starving especially if we had had a little drink of a bottle of beer or me and my mates had had a few swigs from a bottle of wine at somebody's house while playing a bit of music, or even while sat on a school roof. We were never drunk but we could easily be feeling the effect of a small bevy. Once I got home and into the back kitchen I could smell the cooked meat and the smell was tantalising. The smell made my taste buds tingle and my mouth water. I would on numerous occasions try to bypass the oven and get quickly up the stairs but I usually failed and I was drawn to the waiting meat. I loved meat and it was my favourite food now that I was throwing a few bob in to my Ma's purse to help get better food on our table. What I used to do was open the oven door and pull the roasting dish out. With the gas being out for a few hours and the oven now being cold the dripping had formed a hard white layer at the bottom of the dish. The meat joint was stuck in this thick fat to make a solid lump of joint and dripping. I would get the meat in my hand and pull it straight out of the dripping without breaking any of the dripping edges leaving a perfect gap where the meat had laid. I would then get the carving knife and cut a half-inch thick slice of meat off the bottom of the joint and carefully but the joint back into the gap so that you didn't even know it had been moved. I would then put a bit of salt on the meat and get a round of bread from the pantry and wolf it down as quick as I could before going to bed with a belly full of meat. My three brothers would have been in the bed for hours and it would be nice and warm when I got in and in no time at all I would be fast asleep, with nobody knowing what I had been up to.

One Saturday I had had a little more to drink than normal and when I got home and into the kitchen I started with my usual routine. When I opened the oven I saw a lovely piece of beef sat in the dripping. I pulled out the beef and cut a good inch off the bottom before placing it back in the dish. I was that hungry that after eating it and starting out of the kitchen the hunger pains were that bad that I was stopped in my tracks. The meat was talking to me in the oven and my belly was talking back, they were having a right old conversation and I was still hungry. I went back thinking I would have another small piece of it, so went back and cut another thick slice off the bottom. I put some salt on it and ate the meat savouring its delicious taste. With the meat being part cooked it was done a lovely medium rare and this English beef seemed to be perfect just as it was. Well that's it I thought I couldn't take any more even though I was being tempted. I decided to throw everything to the fuckin' wind and have one last slice cutting the joint right down leaving only one small slice of beef left sat on top of the layer of dripping. I must have been more bevied than I thought as there was no way this wouldn't go un-noticed. I went to bed thinking no more of it and was soon fast asleep.

The next minute I thought I was having a nightmare, my mother and father were stood above me screaming blue murder. My Ma had a wooden coat hanger, which she was using to beat me over the back with and my old fella was saying, "You bastard, you've eaten the Sunday joint. You've eaten the Sunday dinner and now there's nothing for us to eat, you bastard." My ma was interjecting "God Charlie why didn't you open a tin of corned beef from the pantry? There's plenty of corned jock in there!" I woke from my daze and found this was reality I was facing and not a nightmare at all. I realised what I had done and my old fella was still screaming at me to get out of the house and how dare I do it, little did he know that it was me who had been putting money in my Ma's purse allowing her to buy the joint in the first place.

I decided that I had had enough of life at home and at school I was being asked by my mate Yank Perry to go to London with him and make our fortunes. Yank was a kid from over the Alt, a Bootleite that had been a staunch enemy of old but was now one of my best mates. The very next day Yank and me along with two girls we knew, Lilly and Mary, decided to run away to London. None of us had been out of Liverpool in our lives but we thought London was the place to go and that we would make it big time in London. I was big for my age and could pass for sixteen easily; this was how old Yank was anyway which made things a bit easier. We set off to seek our fortunes, traveling to London on the train from Lime Street station. Even on our first day in London it became obvious to us that the bright lights of London were not going to shine as bright as we thought. After a couple of days kipping here and there we found a car park that catered solely for coaches or the Charabancs, as they were known then. They had big seats at the back of these coaches and this is where we ended up sleeping. We soon found out that London wasn't easy pickings like it was back in Liverpool and we found it really tough. When the few bob that we had ran out we knew the time was up for our adventure and we should head back home. We could just scrape enough money together for two train tickets home, which of course we gave to the two girls and sent them on their way.

Me and Yank were now walking about London at 1am after a day doing a bit of pilfering, trying to make a few quid and decided to try and hitch hike home. There was only one main road out of London called the Great North Road and that's where we headed. The lorry's used this route to get in and out of the capital and we knew this would be our best chance of thumbing a lift. As we walked we bumped into constable plod (bizzies to us and old bill to the Londoners), we were asked our names but we must have seemed a bit suspicious and they took us in to the station. They asked us all sorts of questions and if we had been in trouble before. I had never been in trouble and so had nothing to worry about but little did I know that Yank had a bit of form for robbery and petty theft. They decided to keep yank in and charge him with loitering with intent, which was a major crime to be accused of and as Yank was sixteen they remanded him in the police cell overnight. They didn't charge me with anything though but I was kept in the next cell to him. The cell had a bench and blanket in their and I thought that spending the rest of the night in the cell would be okay considering I had nowhere else to go and by now it was the early hours of the morning and I was quite content. I decided that only being fourteen; the bizzies would send me home in the morning and would probably even give me the train fare to send me on my way. The next minute I heard the key in the cell door and a copper with his sergeant came in. "Come on you, get the fuck out of here." They pulled me out of the cell and gave me my shoe laces back which they had taken off me before I was allowed into the cell in the first place and pushed me towards the door saying "Now fuck off back to where you came from you scouse bastard. Get back to Liverpool and don't come back." With that I was thrown out of the police station with my protests that I didn't want to leave and had nowhere to go, falling on deaf ears. "But how will I get home?" I shouted, only to get the reply "The same way you fuckin' came!"

They wouldn't even point me in the right direction home, so there I was a fourteen year old kid all on my own on the streets of London at 3am. I was stranded in the middle of nowhere not knowing which way to turn but I was a streetwise kid and this shouldn't be a problem for me, or so I thought. I walked another three or four miles and by now was absolutely shattered, really, really knackered. I decided to sit on somebody's front step and wait for the dawn to come. I hoped that when they opened the door in the morning to collect the milk they would see me and take a little bit of pity on me, hopefully they would give me a buttie to eat and help me on my way home. I was by now walking down a large dark lane and started looking for somewhere to stop as I got even more tired than ever and I was finding it hard to keep my little eyes open. I saw this nice big house on the same side of the road that I was on, and I thought it looked like they must have a few bob. It had a big garden with these hug ornaments in it, I will never forget how magnificent those garden ornaments looked to me as I was half asleep.

I opened the gate and walked down the gravel path leading to steps outside the front of the house. I sat on the steps leaning my head against the front door and started dozing off. As I wasn't lying down my head kept lolling and waking me up with a start, each time I awoke I saw those big ornaments in the lovely garden. The next minute the ornaments seem to be getting nearer and nearer to me. At first I put this down to me being tired and the dim light in the garden playing tricks with my mind, but the horror hit me as I realised the truth behind my predicament. These lovely ornaments were actually monuments and gravestones and I was sat in a graveyard outside a church. It was now about 4am and here I was a kid who still believed in ghosts sat in a graveyard all alone. I tried to make it go away closing my eyes and telling myself that it would be sound and there was nothing to worry about, wishing it would be daylight right now instead of being pitch black. I looked at the gate I had entered by which seemed now so far away through the army of graves that lined the gravel path on each side. I imagined that skeletons would be coming out of those graves and the coffins they held to come and grab me at any moment. I started watching the ground for signs of movement or bony hands appearing digging their way free. I decided I had to get, out so put my head down and ran as fast as I could towards the gate. I expected at every stride that I would be grabbed from behind and dragged below ground to where the skeletons were waiting. I bolted straight over the gate without even opening it I was that scared and didn't stop running or look back until I was a good half-mile away. When I eventually stopped running I collapsed exhausted next to a hedge just trying to get my breath back.

By now the wagons were coming up and down the road and I started thumbing a lift trying to get out of this place and on my way home. A wagon soon pulled up a few yards ahead of me and the Brummy driver asked "Where you going to kid?" I told him I was trying to get back to Liverpool and he said he could take me as far as he could and to jump in. As I got in I could smell the diesel and the engine was keeping a big check blanket inside the cab lovely and warm. I told him what had happened to me and he reassured me that I would be okay. "We will be on the outskirts of Birmingham in an hour or so. Get your head down son and I will wake you up when we are there." He said to me in a reassuring voice. The next thing I knew he woke me up and we were at a roadside café where the driver took me inside and bought me a bacon buttie and a big mug of hot tea. He took me a bit further to a place where he said I would be able to get a lift to Manchester and from there to Liverpool. "Thanks Mr." I shouted "It's alright kid" was all that driver said as he drove away, he turned out to be a decent fella and a lifesaver to me that night. He could have been a perv or a dirty old bastard but he was just a decent fella looking out for a kid in a spot of trouble. It took me nearly two days travelling day and night to get home from London but to cut a long story short I arrived at the fields behind our house. I climbed over the boarded fence at the back of our garden and found the back kitchen door open, I could smell my Ma's cooking on the stove and I thought home sweet home at last. It had seemed an eternity since I left; I was shattered and sore from walking. I went into the back kitchen and saw a big frying pan of bubbling sausages and thick onion gravy ~ sausage and mash was one of my Mam's specialties back then. I couldn't believe how nice it looked, it seemed like heaven to me. I took a fork out of the draw and stuck it in a sausage bubbling in gravy. I knew it would be too hot to eat and probably burn my tongue but I didn't care. Just as I got the sausage towards my mouth my old fella grabbed my wrist. He had come in the back door without me hearing him and said "What the fuck do you want?" as he said this he took the sausage off me and put it back in the pan. "What?" I said. He was angry as he said to me "Ran away from home did you? Fucked off hey? And now you're back with your tail between your legs? Well you can get out now, your not getting back in here!" with that he pushed me out of the back kitchen door and I was left sitting in the back yard not knowing which way to turn. I was nearly crying my eyes out swearing I would get my own back on him when I was older, my Ma who by now had been kicking off with him to let me back in the house sent my brothers out to the field where I had taken refuge with a sausage buttie for me and a shilling for the bus fare up to Kirkby where my elder brother Eddie was now living with his wife and kids. My brother put me up on his couch and I must have slept for almost two days I was that tired. After a day or two our Eddie came in and gave me a bit of a shove "Come on you've been here long enough now. Get out and earn a few quid if you want to stay here. I can't be keeping you for fuck all." He knew I was into thieving and pilfering but also knew he couldn't afford to feed me all the time without some money coming into the house to pay for it, things were still hard.

I knew now I had to get out and start earning, but I needed a small lift to help me on my way. There was only one person I could think of and that was Winnie. This was a new life emerging for me and eventually Winnie would become my villainous mentor.

WINNIE

Winnie to me was the one person I knew at that time in my life who could educate me in the way I wanted to be educated. She had been a survivor during her own life and she seemed to do all right for herself. She was streetwise in every way you could imagine and knew every trick in the trade. This was a woman with great knowledge of the streets as she had told me once that as a young girl she had been forced to live on the streets herself. In the those years it must have been very hard for her, times were hard in my young life but to have lived a generation earlier would have been harder still and Winnie must have been in her late 30's by the time I first met her.

She was a kind and generous woman in her own sort of way but maybe that kindness was shown because she would get rewards for it and deep down Winnie was real modern day Fagin. She knew how to use a lot of psychology on a young kid to get her own way and make them believe everything she told them was for the best. She knew I was wider than the other kids though and so a friendship began between the two of us. It's funny how women all through my life, have always seem to take to me when it comes to trust, and I always seemed to trust them. Our relationship was pure friendship and profit driven, there were no sexual undertones between us as I didn't fancy Winnie at all and she knew it. She knew what sort of kid I was; I only liked girls my own age!

I started questioning her and in return she would start to tell me the best way to be a good thief and how to do different little jobs in order to survive on the streets. My education had now begun. I immediately left my brother Eddies house and moved in with Winnie, she put me up for a good few nights teaching me the tricks of the trade. I slept in the guest room, which was of course on the couch in front of the fire. She fed me and looked after me until my Mam had persuaded my old fella that I should be let back into the house and I could move back home. My mates and me frequented Winnie's house more and more until one day Winnie told me that I didn't need to be grafting with a big gang around me. She said that it was sure to bring it all on top for me when we would eventually be caught and as a big gang all sagging school we were easy to spot. She said I would be better off going out on my own and being different so as not to arouse any suspicion from the bizzies or the school board. In those days the school board were as menacing as the bizzies, they seemed to be everywhere on their regulation bikes looking for kids who were sagging school. Winnie started writing me notes to take in to school and give to the head master, pretending to be my Ma with excuses as to where I had been or where I was going. She was clever you see and knew I couldn't sag school all the time and had to put in an appearance now and then "You've got to keep showing your face Charlie, you don't want them to come looking do you?"

I told Winnie about how I had found a post office savings book ages ago and it was dead easy to draw the cash out of it. She said to me "Well you know where the stamps come from don't you soft lad? The stamps that they put in the books come from the post office and its them you need not the books!" Well this information was new to me but I just retorted confidently "Yeah, I know about all that!" She said that if I went with her up to the post office she would show me how it was done. She said she wouldn't take anything just show me what to do and test my hand under the counter. In those days a metal grill covered the post office counters, with a small rectangular slot at the bottom, a couple of inches high. We end up walking into the post office at Page Moss, Huyton and she asked for some stamps, I think she wanted six pence and three pence stamps that were quite cheap but she also asked for a two bob stamp, which was a lot of money in those days. She knew she could cash the stamp back in later so wouldn't be out of pocket but it showed me some considerable commitment to our cause that day. She told me to watch what they do with the stamp books that were always on the counter behind the grill. What you have to do is get somebody to distract the woman behind the counter then put your hand through the slot and flip open the first cardboard page of the stamp book. You can then hold a sheet of stamps and pull it. As the pages were all perforated at the edges they would come away easily and you may not even have to open the book if you were good enough. She told me that she was well know in the post office we were in and that she would take me to a different place to have a go and see if I could do it. I had already put my arm through the slot so knew I could get most of my arm through and could easily reach the books, she just wouldn't let me do it in that particular post office.

So we went into a different post office and Winnie started chatting away to the woman behind the counter, asking how much it was to send different parcels to a multitude of places. All of a sudden she pressed her shoe heel on my toe and pressed down, not even looking at me or stopping chatting. The woman was now rummaging through draws and I knew this was my signal to have a go. I put my arm through the gap and I couldn't believe it, I had hold of about two or three sheets and with a quick tug they came away in my hand. I quickly brought them back through the gap and folded them up before stuffing them up my jumper sleeve all well down out of sight from the big counter. We both walked out and we must have had about four pounds of stamps, which was a hell of a lot of money at that time. This was when I started hitting post offices big time. I needed a front man though to help me do the jobs so I got my mate Joey Hannagan to come and help me. Winnie knew that Joey was wide too and looked the part so agreed he was a good choice of partner. Every day we did this routine and we made a fortune, but sometimes we stood out a little bit as not quite fitting in, and would have to leave the job empty handed, other times of course we were having it bang off.

I wanted to get more and more knowing I was going up the ladder to becoming fairly big time. Winnie's teachings were rubbing off on me and I was becoming more like her every day. The days of robbing the odd apple to get by had long gone. I had now served my apprenticeship and wanted the rewards for my graft. I was on my way to becoming a proper streetwise kid now plundering and robbing wherever the opportunity arose.

One night, sat in Winnie's talking about the day's events, I told her that we were still getting sussed out and this was hindering our progress even though we had our hair brushed neat and tidy. She said you need to look the part though and at the moment you don't. She asked if I could use our Billy's blazer from his grammar school or rob his badge, but either of those options would soon have been noticed by our Ma so were no good. She then asked if I could get hold of his blazer for a while just so she could have a good look at it and study the badge, this was an easier task and one Sunday when Billy was playing and my Ma was busy cooking I rolled up his blazer and took it round to Winnie as fast as I could on my bike. She studied the badge and the next day she went to town and bought me a black blazer and a badge that was very similar to our Billy's. She also bought a pair of grey flannel pants, shirt and tie for me to complete the outfit. I had started wearing 'longies' and come out of shorts a year earlier but didn't own a pair of grey flannels that would be needed to make me blend in. When I put that outfit on I was completely transformed and I could walk in anywhere and not be stopped by the coppers thinking I was just an urchin. Street urchins were everywhere and the coppers were their archenemies. Since I had graduated away from this crowd walking down the street in my new outfit, I didn't need to run off when I saw a bizzie or dart into an alley way, I could just calmly pass him by without even getting a second glance.

The blazer became my lifesaver for my new career. The stamps were okay but there were other things to try too. Joey didn't need a blazer, as his job was to keep watch and to ensure I could escape if I got into a spot of trouble and a chase broke out. He would often be on his bike and throw himself in front of any pursuing adult making out he had had an accident, blocking their path and making sure I got away. I always fronted the jobs though and our partnership always worked well with us both having a big role to play in the success of the job. We were dead good at this game and everything went well for us both working different jobs for a good two years in full. As this was going on Winnie was happy and my Ma was getting a few quid in her purse and the house was doing okay. She knew what I was doing and what I was up to but couldn't stop me, besides I had tasted the good life and wasn't going back. I thought I couldn't get caught and that nothing would happen to me, I was infallible as we all thought we were. The post offices I had already robbed on my second visit had got wise and the books were a lot further away now even tied up with string or a chain holding them down. We became fucked in Huyton and in most post offices throughout Liverpool finding less and less virgin post offices to rob.

Winnie put the idea of getting a car in my mind saying "It's a pity you can't drive Charlie, cars are a great asset and would mean you could travel further a field." Well the two of us kids on a bike was getting harder to manage the further we went. So at the back of my mind was now the fact that a car would be the best thing for improving our takings. But I still couldn't drive being only fourteen and had no idea how to drive apart from the fact that the gears were somehow in an H shape. Cars were slowly becoming more popular and most early cars had a starter button to get the going but even the ones needing keys were usually left with the keys in the ignition and most of the doors open. It was a usual habit for people to jump out of their car and pop into a shop leaving the engine running just in case somebody wanted to move it while they were gone. The first car I robbed was from the centre of town none of them were locked and some even had the keys in them, it was obvious that it was rare for cars to get robbed at that time. Simply because: 1. There were hardly any cars about to rob in the first place and 2. The working class men didn't know how to drive a car and it was seen as a big achievement to be able to drive with only 1 in 100 men being able to drive. When I was sixteen, I was seen as special by my mates with them often saying, "Can you really drive Charlie? You're not joking are you?" Anyway we picked one we liked the look of, it was a Wolsey, the keys were not there but Winnie had told us that most keys were the same at that time and even a small flat screwdriver would start the car. We used our flat screwdriver and pushed it in the slot, the Wolsey started first time. Our intentions were to drive the car to a remote and desolate spot we knew in Huyton where I could learn to drive the car properly. I had still never driven a car and didn't really have the know how, Winnie had written down for me what to do and what I needed to move in order to get the car moving. I didn't realise that the times when Joey and me had been on the farms and messed about with the farmer's tractor would come in useful now. We had then learnt to push the clutch up and down and to move the gear stick in order to get the tractor to move and cars seemed pretty similar.

I pushed the Wolsey into gear and the car lurched forwards, it was lucky I didn't have to reverse, as I had no idea how that would be done! I drove the car all the way to Huyton a good three or four mile journey in first or second gear. I had no idea what else to do or how to change gears properly. We never got pulled from the bizzies even though Joey was keeping a good look out for any trouble and most of the traffic lights seemed to be in our favour, I was always lucky. The car must have been screaming as we drove at 20 miles per hour in low gear all that way, finally reaching Huyton as a smoking wreck. I had blown the engine and the car never started again, I was gutted. This had been my first disastrous driving experience but little did I know that years later I would become one of the best drivers in Liverpool not just in our gang but in all the criminal fraternity pulling armed robberies in 3.8 litre Jaguar cars or Austin Martins the fastest cars around, I was considered just boss at the driving game. When we were doing these robberies or smash and grabs the 3.8 Jag was our car of choice it was just nailed to the ground and was dead reliable. It could go straight through a shop window and back out again without the passengers even knowing about it.

That first driving lesson didn't go down too well but it wasn't to be my last as when we got back to Winnie and told her about our fiasco she just gave us encouragement to carry on. That was her way, giving guidance and encouragement pushing us further telling us that she knew I could do it and not to give up, its not the end and not to be defeatist. "It's not a problem" she said "just get yourself out and get another one, it will be better this time. Don't give up lads your doing well." So a day or so later we went back and tried again, this time it was an Austin A40, or something, that we took. Remember there were no imported plastic foreign cars at that time, BMW's and Mercedes just didn't exist, and everything was British. All the cars had big steel panels and leather interiors; even the steering wheels were hand crafted. I would need a pillow under my arse in order to just see over the dashboard and get a view of the road ahead. We managed to get the car easily and drove it to the deserted farm on the outskirts of the city where we knew we wouldn't be seen. This time I managed to get into a higher gear and the car was still running fine even by the time we arrived and I was well pleased we had got it there.

The farm had a big old gate, which we opened and once inside we made dead sure it was closed firmly behind us. I was determined to learn how to drive this car; it wasn't going to beat me. I started driving round the field and didn't stop for about two hours, just going round and round learning all the time. I learnt how to change gears properly and how to indicate. I knew how to brake softly and how to do slam on the brakes hard as well as accelerate away again as fast as I could. After this self-taught lesson I got out of the car and stood proudly saying to Joey "I've mastered it Joe, I'm a fuckin' expert driver now and can drive this no problem" and I could. I could drive it well and had picked up the skill in no time at all as the driving instinct must be in my nature. From this point on the car became the greatest asset we had for the robberies ahead of us. We knew the car would be our future and would enable us to move out of town in the times to come and enable us to commit bigger and better robberies.

For now though we would put this future on hold as we still had work to be done where we were and we still had a lot to learn. We covered the car up in an old barn and every other day we would bike up to the barn and top up the petrol in the car from a big petrol can and then drive the car round and round getting more and more skilled every time. I even said to Joey when I was having a blow (rest) that the way I was going on I would end up like Sterling Moss. Eventually I could drive the car blind and knew every switch and gadget the car possessed. I understood the windows, the windscreen wipers, brakes, lights, everything was now known to me and I was its master. We even tinkered under the bonnet with Joey robbing a book to help us get further than we would have done on our own. We studied that book almost as much as the car itself. When we went into town we would see other cars and look with interest for any differences but if we saw an Austin we would say "There's our car, look its not as good as ours is it?" and we would laugh our heads off.

Time passed and as we started being pushed further away to find virgin post offices that we could rob as we had plundered Huyton, Dovecot, Old Swan, Page Moss, Kensington and all the other outlying areas and were now operating right in the heart of the city and pickings were becoming harder. The trouble now was that all the post offices were larger and busier so that if you ended up in a queue with people standing right behind you, then you couldn't do the job and would end up often walking away empty handed. That's when Winnie stepped in again with a little push and a change in direction. Winnie told us to go into the offices and buildings looking about. She said that if we ever found an office empty we should turn it over, as we would always get a cashbox or a draw with money in it or some other valuable items just left lying about. She pushed me on and gave me the confidence that I could get away with this cheeky approach knowing we looked the part, even Joey was now starting to dress smarter and comb his hair more thoroughly in the morning. We looked like two tidy kids together but we always kept our distance from each other when going into anywhere, Joey looking out for me and me keeping an eye out for him. Whenever Joey gave me the nod I would have to get out fast and fuck off, as he would have spotted trouble coming my way. I do remember once Joey commenting that I would never get a pull from the bizzies looking the way I did in the blazer Winnie had made for me and he wondered if he would also look the part if he wore a college school peaked cap. Joey robbed a cap the same day and plopped it on his head to see how he looked. He wore it for about half an hour before I told him to take it off as it made him look like a bad lad. "What do you mean?" he said, "I thought it looked good." "You look fuckin' stupid." I said "First of all you shave now Joe with a good growth coming on, and you've got a kids hat on your head. Your fifteen and a half now and just too big for that stupid hat." Joey laughed and threw the hat over the nearest wall saying "Fuck the hat, its not for me anyway!" We went back to work like ferrets in and out of every door we found, we were living like kings with plenty of readies in our back arse pockets.

Dale Street in the city centre was a good haunt for offices; all the gents wore pin stripes and bowler hats looking like they were all keeping the world moving on their own. We of course were down 'on the mooch' looking for opportunities that would come our way, I could smell money and so could Joey. We used to go into the big buildings in that part of town, the Liver Building, the India Buildings, the Town Hall Buildings, the Cunard Building anywhere that looked impressive ~ Liverpool has some beautiful old buildings. I would have my blazer on and we would never get stopped from going in anywhere. On advice from Winnie I always carried a satchel or a small brown leather briefcase to ensure I wouldn't get a pull and to make my outfit even more convincing in these higher profile buildings. We would go into the buildings and up the stairs looking for opportunity, Joey trailing behind me trying door handles and looking through windows. "Shh" went his signal "There's a door open over here Charlie there's nobody inside" I would then dive in and have a 'mooch' about while Joey kept nix outside. We were doing a form of sneak thieving, which became big business for a lot of scousers years later but we were ahead of the game. I would quickly open the doors of cupboards and draws looking for anything interesting, if I found a cash box I would open it up sometimes finding just a few coins other times finding rolls of notes. I would stuff the takings in my pockets and we would leave the building without raising and suspicion, we tried to target lunch hours when the offices were quieter but never stuck about longer than we needed to. This was a good earner for a few weeks and if I ever got challenged I would say I was looking for my dad who worked in an office a couple of floors away, I would have memorised a company name and they would always just point me in the direction of where my dad was meant to work. I would thank them profusely for their directions and looking the part casually went on my way.

One day when I arrived at Winnie's house with the stash from the previous days work she introduced me to Ray, a fella she knew, saying "Ray's got a little job for you Charlie". He must have been around her age, dressed in a suit and tie with a black pencil thin moustache. He looked a bit slimy to me but I think he was probably giving Winnie one. He had all the hallmarks of a right ponce. Apparently he knew where there was a lot of money stashed but couldn't do the job himself, as he knew the fella it belonged to; in fact he was a mate. What a mate he was!

The fella was supposed to be dead tight and once a week he counted the takings from the business he owned on a big table in his office. He obviously took great pleasure in counting his money and enjoyed his weekly task. There was a bit of problem though as he never left the office when the money was there. "What about when he goes for lunch? Me and Joey will hang about and wait for him before diving in as normal!" I said. "Well that's the problem" he answered "you would have to sit off and wait a long time and it may take weeks of waiting before you got a chance and even then you would have to time it really well." Winnie butted in "He does have a girlfriend across the way in another office block, if that's any help?" Ray continued "Yeah, he fancies himself as a ladies man and he's always touching the girls up who work there too."

I told him we would go and way the place up, so the next day, Thursday, we went down to the place knowing the money wouldn't be there till the Friday. We just wanted to case the place up and see what was what. We did our usual routine walking along the corridors trying doors until we came to the office we needed. We mooched about waiting to see if he left for lunch. Eventually the fella did leave and went across the road to a different office block, presumably to see his girlfriend. As he walked down the isle in the office I saw him touch a young girls arse, she turned round giving him an evil glare. I could see he was a predator and if about today would probably be prosecuted for sexual harassment. After seeing him leave with a young girl and walk down the road we decided we had seen enough and left to consider our plan. The next day we went down again to see if he would leave the cash over lunchtime and to see how much dough we were dealing with. We could see through the glass partition all the cash on the table.

"Just have a look at the readies on that table Charlie," Joey said, "just clock the readies over there, there's bundles and bundles of dough." Joey and me sat off waiting for our chance, but the fella didn't move all day and eventually a security guard came and took the cash away in a leather satchel. Well we weren't in the sort of league yet to do an armed robbery or a snatch on anybody so we just had to watch the guard walk away with our dough.

All week I was thinking about how we could get that knob-head out of his office so we could have is takings away. At one time I was thinking of just opening the door and grabbing a bundle of the cash, but I knew I would only be able to get a small fraction of the cash that was available. I wanted the lot and carried on thinking. I thought about telling him that somebody wanted him in a different office, but if he rang through to check then that would have given our game away. I eventually came up with the final solution that I knew would get him out of the office but I knew it would mean taking a massive chance and was dead risky.

I knew he thought he was a right ladies man and a jack the lad, so I told Joey I was going to go into the office and front up to him accusing him of harassing my sister, by feeling her arse and trying to grope her. "You be ready with a big bag under your arm Joe and when I get him out of the office you get in and grab all the money you can before leaving through the back staircase." I knew I was lucky, and knew my plan would work.

The next Friday we went along and outside the office we could see him there with the readies. We couldn't believe our luck that his routine hadn't changed; we were dead excited and buzzing like fuck. "Get ready Joe. Just watch this and be ready to move." I was going to stick my neck out here. I still had my blazer on and looked the part so confidently walked right into his office. "Yes, can I help you?" he asked in an alarmed voice, obviously not too happy about me being in his office with all that dough on the table. "As a matter of fact you can. Is your name Bill?" I answered. "Yes I'm Bill!" he said. I put both my hands on his office desk and leaned right across to face him and said, "Listen, I'm the brother of one of the girls in the office block over there." "Oh yeah, how can I help you?" he said now inquisitively listening to what I was going to say. "Well you can't help me really, you're just a dirty old man as far as I'm concerned, you've been touching up my sister over there, you've grabbed her arse and been harassing her." "What do you mean? I have not!" he retorted. "You have you dirty old perve " I shouted and with that slapped him as hard as I could across his face with my open palm. He sat up quick and shouted "You little bastard, you little bastard!" obviously shaken at what I had just done to him. "I'm sorry, I'm sorry" I replied trying to luck scared and regretting my actions "ah fuck you anyway!" was the last thing I said to him as he jumped from his desk and started to chase me. I knew he couldn't catch me but I needed to make him think he could so that he would give chase as I left his office. I stayed in what he thought was a reachable distance until we were well away and I knew Joey would have dived in the office and copped for the readies. He eventually stopped chasing me, probably having second thoughts about his money being left in his office unattended, but it was too late as we had copped it good style. Nearly seven hundred quid, a very nice touch in those days.

We had a problem though when we got back to Winnie's house. The Ray Fella wanted a big chop and so did Winnie both trying to make a three way split. Joey and me were having none of it, as we wanted it split fifty-fifty. As the saying goes 'there's no honour amongst thieves'. Joey and me refused to do a three way split and standing on our toes to look bigger we told Ray how it was going to be. "You and Winnie are going to get half, and me and Joey are going to get half, so don't be trying it on with us. I knew he was a slimy bastard as soon as I had set eyes on him and he must have been scheming with Winnie all along. I was a bit disappointed with Winnie that day but it put me on my guard with her from then on.

After that job it was really getting on top and the offices were now getting hammered. We knew the game couldn't last much longer as they new that there were two college kids hanging about and it was getting harder to go un-noticed on school days. The end came when we were in one of the buildings on a corridor full of offices with Joey looking through the windows on one side and me on the other. Joe suddenly said "Shh, shh, Charlie come here quick, over here Charlie, I've just seen a safe in that office over there and the man has just left and gone into the office next door, he's left the fuckin' safe open though! Hurry up. Get in there quick and have a look." "Alright" I said "but keep a good look out for me this could come on top as there's no way out of there if I go in." "You'll be dead sound, I'm with you all the way, get in." he assured me and so I went in to the office. I had to get down low on all fours as anybody passing could see me through the big window facing the corridor outside. I could see the safe straight away; it was a big old green Milliners safe with a brass keyhole in it. The big thick door was slightly ajar and I pulled it open. I could see two bags which I quickly took and was trying to open the locked draws when Joey knocked on the window and mouthed to me "Hurry up ." "Is anybody coming?" I mouthed back. "No but don't be long!" he said. The only other thing in the safe was a small leather wallet, which I stuffed in my pocket before quickly opening one of the bags. It was full of paper money and I knew we had had a good touch and decided to get out fast. Just as I was going out Joey knocked on the window "He's back!" and walked away so as not to get a pull himself. I was still on all fours and hid behind a desk. The man came in and sat at the desk with the safe in it and slowly looked at the open door, being a bit nervous my leg hit a chair and made a small noise. His head darted about and looked over at where I was hiding quickly spotting me crouching on the floor. "HEY, HEY, HEY, WHAT ARE YOU DOING?" he shouted in a posh voice, "HOW DARE YOU! COME HERE YOU LITTLE…." With these words ringing in my ears and unwilling to drop the cash I ran out of the office and the chase was on. We ran down staircases and Joey was right behind me with the man someway behind him still shouting. I knew we would be in trouble trying to get past the commissionaire on the door and as we approached him at full pelt dressed as two posh kids I shouted to Joey "I bet you cant catch me, I bet you cant catch me, I'll beat you to that shop!" The commissionaire looked bamboozled at what he was seeing and when Joey shouted back "I'll beat you, I'll beat you, I'm faster than you, just wait and see" We ran straight passed the commissionaire through the doors and into the street. We didn't stop running though and could hear all the commotion behind us and nervously laughed at the confusion that we had left behind, but after what we had just been through it was no laughing matter. Not for me anyway!

It was in the Liverpool Echo that night about sneak thieves on the loose in Liverpool city centre and two young men were seen running out of the building with the contents of a safe and an undisclosed amount: but we knew the amount - nearly a grand. It even warned the readers that the robberies were happening over lunch times and that they should keep their doors locked. This was the end it seemed of this game but we had done very well out of it and this last touch was our best one yet.

We eventually went to Winnie and showed her our goodies from the safe but to our surprise she didn't seem interested in the cash, which was, when split up, nearly three hundred pounds each. Instead, inside the leather wallet she found two diamond rings that she just couldn't put down. We could see they were important but Joey cottoned on faster than me. Winnie's eyes were twinkling as she looked at the diamond engagement rings. "They're worth a few quid aren't they Winnie?" Joey said. "Oh I don't know lad. I'll have to get my man to look at them; I'm not sure" she replied. "But we know they're worth money Winnie!" Joey wasn't letting her get away with anything by now. "Yeah they're worth a few quid Joey but we need to get them valued." Winnie didn't want to let us know that we had stumbled onto a good thing here but Joey persisted "They're worth a lot of money them, Winnie. Don't try and blag us!" With Winnie having much more knowledge of jewellery than either Joey or me it became a standoff and a stalemate soon developed. I came to the rescue though and got everybody round the table to sort it out. "Look Winnie, were willing to share everything with you now cos you've been really good to us, but don't try and rip us off from now on! No more ripping off, you know the score with us now Win." We could see the look on her face as she warmed to me and thought to herself, 'well I've got these two working hard now and I don't want to kill the goose that lays the golden egg'. We knew we didn't really need her now and soon we would have outgrown her, becoming professionals and experts in what we did.

Winnie surprised us then with one of the greatest ideas I have ever encountered in my life. She said "I'm going to teach you something now Charlie that nobody knows about and we can all make plenty of money out of it. Forget the offices and post offices now as they are coming on top, and you're not quite ready to move out of town yet. What I'm going to show you is one of the best moves I know. I'll let you in on it just so long as I keep getting my chop."

We swore allegiance to one another and I swore my undying loyalties to her saying we would never try anything on. Winnie then asked me to call round the next day without Joey. There was never any hard feelings though, as Joe knew he wasn't as skilled as me at the game and was happy to take a back seat and play his own role. When I went into the house it was the same old routine that Winnie always did. "Are you alright Charlie? Had anything to eat today?" She wasn't going to give me anything it was just a bit of chat to show willing and build a bond. I had already eaten as food was plentiful in our house now and none of us were hungry anymore. She asked me to sit down and went into her back kitchen. When she returned she was carrying a small wooden box, which she placed on the table in front of me. She opened the box and pulled out a black jewellery pad, it was just a piece of card covered in velvet with rows of rings in it. It looked just like the real displays in a jeweller's window. In it were all types of rings, wedding rings, diamond rings and ornate dress rings all displayed to their best advantage on the card. I don't know where she got those rings from; they must have been what she was saving up with for her pension or something. She said, "See this Charlie, this is what we want now, this is where the money is and you'd be better off going into Jewellery shops. I've got a good out for the rings and you will know how much they are worth when you get them so nobody will be ripping anybody off."

She started to tell me what I had to do by making me promise not to go for the too high priced rings as that can make the jeweller suspicious with you only being a kid and bring it on top. What I needed to do was pretend to be a schoolboy in love and choosing an engagement ring for my sweetheart as now you are sixteen (I looked sixteen by now even though I was only fourteen and a half) and would like to get engaged. She said it was important for me to give them the patter and make them believe I was a sweet kid in love; it would be easier if I chose a female assistant, as they are a bit soppier than the fellas. She told me that I would look the part as long as I always wore a clean white shirt and put a tie on with my slacks and blazer and would get away with it easy. She then said "Watch this Charlie, this is how its done!" She pretended to be the shopper and I was the jeweller. She put the pad down on the table and said "I've spotted this pad in the window as the one I want to look at and the jeweller will go and get it for me to have a closer look." She told me that I should always choose a pad that had plenty of empty slots on it and never go for an almost full pad as this helped bamboozle the shop assistant. I should keep the patter up saying things like me and my girlfriend are saving up and at one time were even thinking of running away to Gretna Green but both sets of parents would be upset and we couldn't put them through that. It was of course all for show in order to put the assistant at ease and take her look away from me. She said, "Watch what I do once the pad is placed in front of me." then she started her routine.

"Ohh aren't they lovely, I really like that one there" all the time not touching the rings but looking at them in awe and pointing at the one she had chosen. "Can I have a look at it please?" She then picked up the ring very carefully and examined it close "It is beautiful isn't it, I think this may be the one but I will need to go home and think about it." She then carefully places the ring back down holding it between her thumb and index finger. As she put the ring back down in its place her little finger curled through a ring below in on the pad and the second ring was quickly held in the palm of her hand where nobody could see. The jeweller would only see her put the ring she was looking at back very carefully and with the new ring in her hand she turned and walked away from me. "See it's dead easy Charlie, but you need to practice." After she had shown me the routine I knew I could do it and thought it looked so easy. We had a little talk about things and she started to quiz me about what I wanted to do when I was older. "Want to get a nice job Charlie?" "You must be joking I'm sticking to this game." This life was just too good to turn away from and I was never going to look back ever again. She then gave me some advice I would never forget. "Don't be hasty into anything Charlie, If anything doesn't look right don't do it. Don't step out of line if it doesn't feel right, just walk away and stay free to thieve another day."

Those words always stuck with me and I often took her advice. Once years later I was doing a wages robbery on a factory over the other side of the Mersey. What I didn't know was that there was an enemy in the camp and one of the gang I was working with was a police informer. The police in Liverpool at that time were after me and I was a wanted man as a high profile criminal. The police would do anything to nail me, as they could never catch me doing anything wrong. They knew I was usually the man in the lead and normally carried a gun on the job, with my preference being a sawn off shotgun. The night before the job the firm was sat about making plans, and since nobody wanted to carry the gun, as it took nerve to carry the gun knowing that if you got caught the one with the gun would get a lot more bird than the others, I agreed that was my part. The snide in the camp didn't know me properly and underestimated me quite badly. Although he knew I was to use the gun and that we were going in two cars, him and two fellas in one car and me with two of my trusted mates in another, what he didn't know was that it didn't smell right to me. The next morning I just had this feeling and my sixth sense was telling me something was up. I didn't like this new fella who had just been brought in for the job and knew very little about him, I would normally like to know somebody's pedigree and credentials but on this occasion didn't. I knew I was under surveillance at the time and the police were determined to get me even if that meant fitting me up.

I said to the two lads that I was graftin' with to make their own way over there in the car without me. Telling them that since I was carrying the shooter if we got caught it would be a lot better for them if I wasn't with them. It was all down to me then. I told them I was uneasy about the job, but they assured me all would be okay, not to worry and that I may have been getting a bit paranoid. I knew I was taking a bigger risk than them, as my part was to stand by the gates and if the bizzies just happened to come on the scene even if there were twenty men were running at us I would still try and fend them off with the shotgun. I would shoot low and because the gun was sawn off the cartridge would pepper the bizzies at a really low level, covering a large area but not killing anyone. I wasn't scared of doing this even though I had never shot anybody in my life at that time. I had on past armed blags let the gun go every now and then to scare people and maybe fire into a ceiling to calm things down but I had never aimed the gun at anybody and shot them. I dismantled the shotgun up into small pieces and put them into a haversack that I would carry as part of my workers uniform to go with my donkey jacket, cap, jeans and boots I was wearing and made my way by train across the water. The two cars drove practically on top of the job and sat waiting while it took me some time to get there, as I walked to the job I happened to walk down the road we had planned to use as our escape route and what should I see there but a cop car. Not just one though a little further down was another cop car, just like a roadblock. Even further down I saw even more of the filth and I knew it was a set-up.

I knew where my mates would be parked waiting for me, and also that the coppers couldn't know who they were. I was certain they knew me though and would be looking for me arriving in a big car at speed and then jumping out with a shooter. They didn't see me casually walking down the street passed them, in fact one bizzie got out of his car and started chatting to another copper on his radio so I knew they hadn't recognised me. I saw my mate's car parked a few streets away and went straight up to them and tapped on the window, "Get out of here now its on top, it's a set up!" I carried straight on with my haversack and made my way down a back alley. I put the pieces of the gun in a few different bins and made my way back home. I walked out of that trap as a result of Winnie's wise words all those years before and I often thought of Winnie when I was about to do an armed robbery. The fella who I suspected set me up left town that night and never came back so my suspicions were dead bang on.

The weekend before I was to attempt getting my first ring I stayed at Winnie's all Saturday and Sunday practicing. We kept going over and over it together, knowing I was already good enough to pull of the job. I felt confident in my appearance, the story I was going to tell and the slight of hand needed to get the ring itself. I had an angels face and people said I looked like butter wouldn't melt in my mouth, little did people realise that I was a wolf in sheep's clothing. Underneath my masquerade I was turning into a real villain and I couldn't wait for Monday morning to come round and the shops in town to open. Winnie told me that it was best not to go first thing in the morning but to wait until the hustle and bustle of town was well underway and the shop would be busier. Winnie came with me on that day, not going into the shop with me but instead lurking about looking in other local shop windows, waiting to see if I could pull it off.

I selected one of the main jewellers in the city centre there were many to choose from with Boodle and Dunthorne, Samuels, Pikes and Miltons being just a few. Each jewellery shop seemed to somehow specialise in different types of jewellery but they all sold engagement rings. Getting engaged was a very big thing in the 1950's and everybody made a fuss over young couples in love. All the films seemed to have happy endings with the leading lady being proposed to and a big engagement ring being slid on her finger. I was brimming with confidence when I walked into the shop and there wasn't an ounce of fear in me. I was ready for this moment and had worked hard to get here. I had my outfit on and a week before had added the finishing touch, we had robbed a couple of top-notch Parker pens which I now proudly displayed one of in my blazer top pocket. It was considered very impressive to wear a blazer and carry a nice pen. Most jewellers were just shopkeepers and assistants although on rare occasions the shop owner would work in the shop too. It was just before lunchtime when I decided it was time to hit the shop. I had let the assistant take a good look at me as I pondered in awe in the shop window, scratching my head and looking bewildered at all the rings on display. I knew a male assistant had spotted my act and was watching me as I started to walk away from the shop before returning again and looking once more longingly at the rings. He must have been watching me through the window and thinking I was a soppy young kid looking at the engagement rings with an 'if only she'd say yes' look on my face.

I was in luck though as there were a lot of pads there with rings missing but I didn't want to go overboard and pick a too expensive ring "If you pick one too expensive it will bring it on top Charlie." Winnie's words were now ringing in my ears as I stood deciding which tray and ring to take. I memorised which pad I wanted and entered the shop looking as shy, bewildered and out of my depth as I could. I wanted the assistant to feel sorry for me and think it was my first time in a jewellery shop, which of course it was! I didn't cause them any cause for concern as I walked in, unlike the thieves of today some hooded who all look like thugs with skinheads and a face full of tattoos. I just looked like a pleasant young schoolboy looking for a romantic ring for my girlfriend and most people were romantics at heart in those days and suspected nothing out of the ordinary.

"Hello young sir." Said the male assistant that greeted me as I walked in. Well I wanted a female assistant as Winnie had instructed but it was too late now he had seen me in the window and now wanted to serve me. Trust me to get a bloke on my first time. "Can I help you at all?" He said. "Well I'm saving up to be engaged to my girlfriend. We often talk about it when we go to the pictures and out on dates." I said trying my best to look embarrassed at even being there. "It's okay son, you can open up to me, after all I was your age once" he said, trying hard to put me at ease and obviously being led right into my trap. I was leading him better than I would a woman and he started giving me some chat and friendly advice. Eventually he asked me what I had seen and I told him which tray the ring I was looking at was on. He disappeared to the window and brought it back placing the tray right in front of me on the big glass counter just like Winnie had said he would. "Which one were you thinking of?" He asked. "I was looking at this one here" I replied "but now I like the look of that solitaire just above it." The ring I was going to select was forty pounds but the solitaire I had jumped in with was fifty-five and I thought I may have blown it by going for a too expensive ring. My mind now raced away from me, why had I done that, why had I

124

gone for the more expensive ring but since there were rings worth hundreds of pounds on the same tray I soon talked myself into the fact that it was still going well. "Well they are both lovely sir. What price range were you thinking of?" "I've got quite a lot saved up and I can almost afford this tiered forty pounds ring here, I will have the money for that very soon now but that solitaire is just so nice. My girlfriend has often said that she loves solitaires and that one just stands out to me." As I said this all the rings on the tray started to sparkle at me and their brightness almost overcame me. The assistant said that maybe we could come to some sort of arrangement over the solitaire, paying weekly in instalments and offering other tempting payment options.

"Could I just have a look please?" I asked. "Certainly sir, take your time." The assistant had no fears over me at all and I was now in his trust. I picked up the tiered ring first and looked at it carefully. I put it back in the pad slowly without taking another ring and then carefully picked up the solitaire. I stared at it in awe holding it up to the light to try and see it better. As I had picked up the solitaire I also picked up the tray in my other hand, I was now stood holding the tray loosely in my left hand while I gazed at the diamond ring I held in my right. By now he doesn't seem interested in what I'm doing with my fingers or hands and just seems happy deep in thought about my romantic story. I started getting excited now as I knew I could do it and there was a ring on the pad in perfect position. I put the solitaire ring back in the tray at the same time scooping my chosen prize into my waiting palm. I put the tray down firmly with both hands and let my arms drop to my sides. "I'll have to think about which ring I really want." I said. "Is this pad always in the window as I would like to get my girlfriend to come and look at the pad through the window to see which one she picks out. She only works in one of the offices across the road and she's ever so excited too." "You go away son and have a think about it together. I wish you the best of luck. What's your girlfriends name?" "Sandra." I replied. This was the first name that came into my head and had no relevance at all. People were milling about the shop by now and I casually walked out of the shop and down the road with the ring pressed firmly in my hand. Winnie was looking in a shop window a couple of doors away and I walked past her without making a sound. She turned and ambled along the street behind me as if we were total strangers. A couple of streets away when I showed her the ring her eyes lit up and she just said "Great Charlie, were in business now and this is going to be great." With that we got the bus back to her house.

When we got into her house she said how beautiful it was and that she already had a buyer lined up for it. She also showed me what she did with all the rings she got, taking me into her back kitchen and filling a bowl with lukewarm water form her brass tap and put the bowl on her wooden draining board. She added some soap and mixed it up before taking out a very small brush and scrubbing the ring. "Look at the sparkle on that Charlie." She said. She loved jewellery and if ever there was a woman that liked diamonds and gold it was Winnie, she was like a typical magpie and needed those rings just as much as I needed the money.

"I'll have this sold by tomorrow" she said "are we going fifty-fifty on this Charlie? You know I won't get forty pounds for it don't you. It's only worth half the price it would be in a shop." I wished

I had Joey with me now to help me negotiate with her, I wasn't sure if she was at the other business now and trying to blag me. I had to ensure that next time I was sure she wasn't ripping me off so told her that I needed Joey to start coming with me in case there was a bad off man, working as a team just like we used to. I told her that she couldn't do what I needed and anyway she had a lot more to loose than Joey and me. Winnie being selfish only wanted to split the takings between two of us instead of three if Joey joined in. She didn't like the idea but reluctantly agreed knowing it was going to be my way or no way. I was learning fast now and started to manipulate both Joey and Winnie to get more and more my own way, they both needed me and relied upon me knowing I was bringing in the money on their behalf. We battered Liverpool for quite some time and we robbed many, many rings over a couple of months.

After this period I started to worry that the ring robberies were getting too well known and that I would soon be I.D'd and the job would be on top for me. This now seemed a big chance to take for just one ring, especially as we thought my face might be getting put on offer and I could come badly unstuck. Inevitably I started to think of other ways to get the money. I was fourteen and a half and leaving school in six months time and needed to increase my earnings accordingly. I knew I was going to be at it big time and jewellery shops were going to give me a good earner, with little security and nobody else targeting them it seemed like an ideal opportunity. I decided to do one last shop before I gave this sort of game up. I was now grafting with Yank Perry. He had a hard background, with plenty of bottle, and was in fact one of my old Bootleite enemies from over the Alt. He even said he had a better fence who would buy more rings off us, and give a better price for them than Winnie. I told Yank I was doing one last job and to meet me on his bike for a quick off man. I told him I was going to hit a big jeweller in town that sold top class jewellery compared to a lot of the other shops. He had to be ready as I was going to be running out of that jewellers shop as fast as I could and be heading Yanks way with a full tray of rings. Yank was to be positioned down a small back street a few yards away facing towards me and as I ran by him I would give him the tray and he would slot it down his jumper. He could then ride towards the crowd that was chasing me, looking like he was just caught up in all the commotion.

I went into the jewellers knowing it would be my last time doing this sort of graft and that I had to make it worthwhile. This job gave me an insight into my later years with a philosophy of 'all or nothing' and I might as well take twenty rings as just one. I had one last go at this game, wearing my lucky blazer, shirt and tie. I even put some Brylcream on my hair and, having pressed my grey flannels with the big old metal iron and a damp cloth, making sure the creases down the front were immaculate, I was well groomed and fronted up to the shop assistant looking my best. I started my chat up line and told her all the usual things and then asked to see the tray of rings out of the window. The female assistant must only have been about eighteen and was 'made up' with my story and the look of young love; she would probably have been a hopeless romantic herself. I had the tray in my hands and knew the time was almost upon me and I started to worry. The glass counter the girl was behind went all the way round the shop; in those days there were never grills, cameras or alarms in the shops. It was just down to me and my bottle, should I or shouldn't I? Maybe a copper will come in just as I start to run? Maybe a passer buy will grab me or pounce on me as I leave the shop? Maybe I couldn't run fast enough to make my escape? I was trying to control my nerves as the glittering rings shone up at me, they must have been worth at least three thousand pounds. I decided to take the chance and said to the girl "There very nice them, I will just have to see my girlfriend and see if she would like one of theses." "There very expensive" she said. "Well my dad has his own haulage business and my mum is a school teacher so I don't think it will be a problem" I replied, which must have been very impressive to her. I was still holding the tray and now my gaze hit the door and I saw my opportunity and ran. I hit the door running and pulled the big brass door handle to make my escape. I was gone in a flash!

Round the corner our getaway was waiting, a bike! No car or van, not even a motorbike. The first real time I would need a proper wheel man and all we had was a pushbike with a fuckin' kid on it. I ran past Yank and slotted him the tray, which he stuffed down his jumper and pedalled like the clappers. I ran down the alleyway and emerged onto the main street. The 10B tram to Huyton had just pulled away and was heading down the street so I decided to leg it. You often see people running for a tram and jumping on it so there was nothing unusual about my actions as I caught the tram, jumping on the back platform and holding on to the silver pole. "You almost missed it there son didn't yer!" said the conductor to me not knowing how lucky I was to have been on the tram at all. I sat upstairs knowing that the tram had to past the jewellers I had just robbed. There were a few people outside scratching their heads and what looked like the manager stood with his hands on his hips and glasses on his forehead just looking up and down in bewilderment. I kept my face sideways to them on the tram not letting them see my face as we passed them by.

Little did I know that this would be repeated in history, as years later my gang and me were sizing up a bank for an armed robbery. It was situated in a town centre not too far away from Liverpool. Our main concern was how to get the money away without being caught as the police station wasn't very far away and we knew there would be road blocks in position before we could get out after the robbery and the whole thing would be right on top for us. We had to rule out cars, which were our normal getaway vehicle as screaming cars, being driven at high speeds through the back roads would mean certain capture. What I suggested was that one car dropped us off outside the bank while another lie in wait a good few miles away and beyond any police road blocks that may be set. I said that we should use a pedal bike to get the money out of the town. At first I was laughed at, "Are you serious Charlie? A fuckin' bike what are you on about? You must be joking!" I said to them "I know it will work!" and told them I had done it years before as a kid and that the same routine would work again. One of them piped up "Its not 1953 now you know Charlie, were talking about a proper bit of graft here worth thousands. It's a bit iffy!" But when I explained the plan that Kenny, one of our men, would get on the bike looking the part, dressed as an old workman on his way home from work and he would cycle out of town with the cash in his haversack they all agreed that nobody would stop him and that the bizzies wouldn't suspect a thing. I had the sixth sense still and knew the plan would work, I still lived by the rule instilled into me by Winnie that if it didn't feel right don't do it, but this felt dead right.

On the day of the robbery we were dropped off outside the bank and the blag went perfectly. We escaped out of the bank to the waiting car in the nearby car park. We put the cash on the ground next to the car and filled up Kenny's long haversack, which he put on his back and quickly peddled away. He looked the part even down to the last detail. He had got a donkey jacket with the plastic strips across the shoulders, an old flat cap and dirty steel toe capped boots. He peddled straight through all the roadblocks and never even got a pull once. We of course ditched the car just round the corner, split up and took busses out of town. I remember sitting on the top deck of the bus seeing all the commotion and our trail of destruction out of the window just like all those years before. It was eight miles to the safe house where the slaughter was taking place and Kenny was soon there with the readies just like I had planned.

Just like the bank robbery our childhood jewellery robbery was the talk of the town and everybody knew what had happened. Yank and me made eight hundred pounds for that tray of rings taking four hundred each ~ a lot of money then, but can you imagine what the fence made for himself after paying us out. This was the most money I had ever had; at that time you could buy a semi-detached house with eight hundred pounds. I wasn't quite fifteen yet but knew I was hitting the big time and nothing was going to stop me!

Above My younger brother Billy and me in our American Navy Sailor Suits.

Notice the writing on our hats. I am 4 and Billy is 2. Its 1944.

Top: My Ma on far left, having a laugh for a change with some of her friends in 1950. In those years most married women were kept down by their selfish husbands.

Bottom Left: My beautiful sister Delia. I think deep down out of all her brothers I was her favourite

Bottom Right: My oldest brother Eddie in 1947. This isn't a man you could tell a secret to, as he would let the world know.

Top Left: My two younger brothers Jimmy and Joe. Our Jimmy was always in awe of me, his bigger brother, especially of the stories I used to tell. In later years he became my favourite brother and his loyalties to me were beyond compare.

Top Right: My old fella on the left, outside the Liver Buildings.

Bottom Left: My Ma's side of the family in 1947. I classed them tuppenny toffs, you can see how smarmy they were by the looks on their faces.

Bottom Right: My Ma's posh brother Charlie who I was named after. He would turn in his grave if he knew the way I turned out.

Top Left: This photograph was taken in 1942. Here he is ready to fight the Germans emerging from the camouflaged air raid shelter behind him.

Top Right: Neighbours kids playing in their backyard. Note the dolly tub and dolly peg hanging on the wall. These were used instead of today's modern washing machines.

Bottom Left: Little Tommy in his tin bath after a hard day's riding on his bike.

Bottom Middle: The Linsky sisters playing on their swing a few doors away from our house.

Bottom Right: Baby and his sister.

THIS PAGE

Top Left: Mrs Stewart and her daughters sitting outside their shelter; good friends and neighbours of ours.

Top Right: Maureen playing in her back garden a few doors down the road.

Middle Left and Bottom: 1940's Liverpool kids. Notice how there was no fear of kids being molested or run over by cars.

Middle Right: Simple toys for a simple way of life; teddy and pram.

Top: Between 1940 and 1945 this was the scene that greeted most Liverpool kids.

Bottom: Air raid shelters, they were everywhere!

All: VE day (Victory in Europe) parties in our road.

Top Left: See me sitting with my waistcoat on just behind Genette Connel aged 5.

All: The parties are over and everything is winding down.

Middle: The grown ups are dancing in the street while I stand watching at the far left.

Top right: Anyone want a cuppa? There were no tea bags then, only stewed tealeaves.

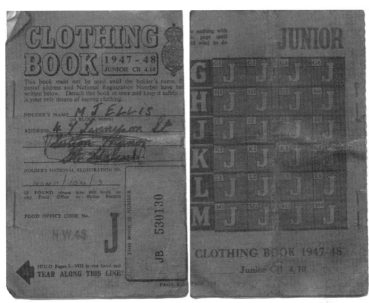

Above: 1947 Clothing book

THIS PAGE

Top Left: Young Liverpool men ready for war.

Top Right: Liverpool lads merchant navy.

Bottom Left: Liverpool soldier proudly holds his child before going to fight in the war. He probably only had a one week pass.

Bottom Middle & Right: More brave souls sending their portraits home.

Top: These young Liverpool men are all brothers who were from the Scottie Road area. Second from the right is Joe Hanson my sister's husband.

Middle: Another gang of Scousers ready to have a go at the Germans. Sadly some never came back.

Bottom: Liverpool lads in the merch during the war. A lot of their ships were torpedoed and sunk by the Germans.

All: War brides

Bottom left: My sister Delia on her wedding day with my old fella.

THIS PAGE

Top Left: These were the Liverpool dolly birds of the 1940's. You can tell from the photo that they were party animals, and living for the day because of the war.

Top Right: Another beautiful young Liverpool woman of the 1940's

Left: Two sisters in their back garden.

Top: Typical 1940's street scene.

Bottom: Women gather for the works photograph.

Top: After the blitz in Bootle, Liverpool. Kids playing where once stood some of their homes.

These people suffered the worst of all the Liverpool bombings - even more so because they lived right on the dock front.

Middle: One of the old trams we used to leg.

Bottom: The Liverpool overhead railway, which the Dockers christened the umbrella. This stretched right across the docks and you could walk for miles, never getting a drop of rain on your head even if it was pouring down. This is the very street where we used to leg on to the Puffin' Billies and wagons to steal our peanuts and brown sugar etc.

All: Liverpool kids after the war in happier times.

Top and Middle Left: The donkey rides in New Brighton.

Middle Right: A gang of Huyton kids in 1948. My mate George Glover can be seen on the right, wearing his short kecks.

Right: Church Street

Above: This is the famous Scotland Road, or Scottie Road, as we would call it. The street stretched right into the city centre and it was fascinating to me as a kid.

If you were to walk down this street on any day of the week, the first thing that hit you would be the aroma of real Liverpool Irish food, such as ribs and cabbage, pea soup made from bacon shanks, and not forgetting the good pans of scouse. On Sundays the menu would change: starting off in the morning with "salt dolly" (salted cod), followed by tasty roast dishes.

There used to be a pub on nearly every corner, mostly full of warm and friendly characters. The majority of the people who lived along Scottie Road were of strong Irish Catholic descent, but there was also a small Italian quarter. Both of these communities got on well together, even marrying into each other's families at times. Both my own brothers, Ged and Jimmy, have sons, Shane and Jamie, who married into the Volante and Ventri families.

Some of these people were good friends of mine and still are to this day.

Top: Dale Street, 1947.

Bottom: Castle Street, 1952.

Both: These two streets, along with Church Street and the rest of the major streets in Liverpool city centre, gave me a good living as a kid. This is where I operated.

I was always dressed as an office boy in my blazer, shirt and tie. Looking at me, with my baby face, you wouldn't have thought butter would melt in my mouth. Under all this masquerade, deep down, I was still just a little scally, darting in and out of all these office buildings like a ferret, raiding their cash drawers and safes.

All: These shops in Huyton gave me a living as a kid. On a routine basis I plundered every one of them.

Top Left: Scottie Road kids on the mooch, as these kids were real streetwise. Note the pram hasn't got a baby in it. I wonder why?

Middle Left: The little village shop in Knowsley, just outside of Liverpool, where I used to rob my sweets and comics from.

Middle Right: This is Pegram's shop, the one I actually worked in before I got sacked for robbing some groceries.

Top: 1948 cars were seldom seen outside a council house. Working class people just couldn't afford to own one. This picture shows neighbours of ours in Huyton. This old Austin car is similar to the one I stole when I was 13 and learnt how to drive in.

Bottom: Gambling was illegal in the 1950's. This typical card school being set up was taken on our back field in Huyton. As a kid I used to be a good lookout, keeping watch for the bizzies coming.

Above: 1940's and 1950's Liverpool factory girls. Life was hard for most working class women. Their wages were lower than a mans even though some of them did the same work. ~ What a liberty!

Note the girl in the background ready to pull her truck up the cobbles. It was pure slavery.

Left: Here I am again just a kid of 13 years (1953) dressed in my famous blazer, shirt, tie and trousers. This outfit enabled me to earn a good living on the streets and kept the bizzies from sussing me out.

Bottom: Taken 6 months later in 1954 with two of my mates, Peter and Joey. Joey is the camera shy one in the middle. Note the lucky blazer is still going strong and by this time we are really bang at it and making plenty.

Above: Winnie.

This woman was my mentor. When I was a kid she showed me the ropes and how to make a living on the streets. Without her expertise I might have ended up in a factory, drudgingly clocking on and off.

God bless you, Winnie, wherever you are - hopefully it's above, rather than below.

1955

I had come a long way since 1945 and in those ten years I had lived as a streetwise kid and sampled money beyond my own dreams. I was still only fifteen and only just about to leave school and was thinking in my own mind, 'What does the future hold for me? What does the future hold for all my mates? What is the next move for us all?' Well I knew exactly what my next move was going to be and there was no going back. We were all soon sitting on the back field behind our house discussing what we were going to do in the future, most of us just about to leave school, some already left. "What are you going to be when you grow up?" Well it was time to answer the question we had asked each other in years gone by. I couldn't believe what most of my mates were planning; Joey my long-term partner in crime had already joined the Merch and put his days of thieving behind him. Peter Hart (Wacker) said he was going down the mines to be a miner, this sounded like slavery to me but he seemed excited about the idea and thought it was going to be a good job. Tommy and Yank were both going straight getting jobs on building sites carrying bricks and learning a trade. Most of the others went on to work in factories and shops trying to become respectable earning a steady wage. The money they were earning was a pittance but I knew that even though I wasn't going to follow them down this path I still needed to put on an act to everyone including my family and needed to get an honest job.

Six of us on leaving school were sent to work in the United Glass Bottles (UGB) factory just out of Liverpool in St Helens. That morning my mates and I were all sitting on the top deck of the bus, which was coming out of Huyton on our way to work. Most of the grown ups were sitting there reading the morning papers. I remember them all discussing Ruth Ellis the last woman who would be executed in England. Her hanging was that very morning and I remember one older fella saying, "That poor girl gets topped in half an hours time." It was headline news, but us being young baby faced kids didn't take much notice at the time.

On that first day I couldn't believe what I saw, getting off the bus all I could see was a clonking noise of the people marching into work. The men with their steel toe capped work boots and cloth caps and the women trudging along in their works trousers and flat-heeled shoes. It was like an organized ant march, everybody marching to work ready to clock on and looking forward to clocking off. I had shudders going down my back as my laughing mates were jostling along, asking each other what they thought the first day was going to be like. I knew that this life wasn't for me and I wasn't happy about being there with them and becoming a kept down peasant like most of our forefathers. On that first day we waited for the yard manager to collect us from the hut we were waiting in. When he arrived he said, "Come on lads I've got you all a job here, pick a truck up each and follow me." We all picked up a two-wheeled truck each and pulled them up the cobbled yard of the factory. All of a sudden I heard giggling and laughter coming from a group of women coming the other way. They were pulling the trucks down the hill we were going up with big wooden boxes (DD's) on them filled with bottles. The women were only in their early twenties with some even still in their late teens, but they were all women to us. They all wore headscarves and vest like sweaters with their pants or skirts, even though it was

May now and getting quite warm. As they pulled their trucks past us, giggling between themselves at this new gang of kids being brought into the factory and led to their slaughter, I could see their hairy armpits. They weren't like the girl of today, well groomed and shaved or waxed, their armpits had big hairy clumps of curly hair under them. The worst were the 'wooly backs' (people from outside of Liverpool) they seemed to have no thought about how they looked and didn't give a fuck. They all just plodded on with their work and this was their way of life and always would be. I couldn't stick at this life and after just three days left the factory never to return, throwing my lunch bag over the wall saying to Joey Tate, Tommy Tate, Tucker Hughes and the other new lads "I've had enough, this isn't the life for me." They couldn't believe I was going, throwing a good job away just three days in was considered mad to them.

I wanted a different path, sampling the best and not becoming a drone working day in day out just to scrape a living together getting a wage packet at the end of each week. I would often bump into the others who had discarded their former lives for an honest job and they would seem discontented when they couldn't afford the things I could. I was bang at it though as Freddy my older brother had just completed his ten-year prison stretch and was now back home. He wanted to go straight back into crime and start earning some real dough. They say prison is a school of learning for criminals and it was just as if his mind had been corrupted someway while he was inside as he had been studying and met a lot of people from out of town. He brought a couple of cockneys to our house and they were talking about safe robberies and a lot of big time stuff. That night when the two cockneys had gone, our Freddy had a quiet chat with me and said that I could jump in with him and his mates if I wanted blowing safes. "Safe blowing? What do you mean?" I asked. Our Freddy started to educate me saying, "Blowing the doors off safes, that's where the real money is kept not in petty cash boxes. When you have one of these jobs away Charlie it is worth taking the chance for, there's a lot more readies involved and people can retire on the money they get from this sort of graft." I knew there was no going back now as he planted it into my young head that this was the big time, and so my life completely changed and I became a truly professional criminal.

EPILOGUE

Looking back was it the right or wrong path, to go and work in those factories or learn an honourable trade? Did I take the wrong path? Well I don't think so, looking at the things I have sampled through life that my mates never got the chance to. Some of my old mates are now sadly dead but some are living in small two up, two down council houses and that was the life they chose, hard working and honest. Me though, I sampled a different life enjoying world cruises, the best cars and expensive jewellery. I've been with beautiful women and had all the best clothes, I remember when we always had a good touch we would sometimes charter a small private plane and fly to Maximes in Paris for lunch, purely to impress our girlfriends. My young life was for living. Money was for spending and there was plenty of it. I know certain men, good men, who were bang into crime and made plenty out of the game. Some have never seen the inside of a police station or a jail. The ones that are still alive have retired now and of course are living comfortably. Who said crime doesn't pay? Well I am not saying crime does pay! I know there are many young lads today that are into crime, but their crimes and my crimes are vastly different. For instance we didn't go out and mug the ordinary man in the street, we only stole from people who could afford it, rich fat cats and the like. I'm not saying all criminals are muggers and there are villains today who still hold the old school principles. Villains who would still go to the aid of an old man getting mugged or a woman getting raped, villains with morals like myself. Maybe there aren't as many as there were though! As far as people taking the right path, working in factories and doing honest work, I have nothing against them whatsoever, and wish good luck to them all.

For maybe ninety percent of villains who take to crime it certainly does not pay, but for the other ten percent, the ones it does pay for are probably just born with luck.

Years later I bumped into some of my mates. Wacker Hart had been down the mines for thirty plus years and he looked like a little old man. Some of the others had been working all their lives on building sites and the elements seemed to have weathered not only their appearance but also the man himself. Some of them had to resort to Zimmer frames and wheel chairs in the end, whereas I am still a fairly fit and healthy man. 'Hard work never kills you' they say. Well I think it would have killed me a long time ago. Thinking about Rowena the gypsy woman all those years ago she certainly blessed me with a lot of luck. Luck I still have with me today.

WHERE DO YOU GO FROM HERE?

Killer

Killer, the international bestseller and the second chapter of Charlie Seiga's epic autobiographical trilogy, continues the story of his life.

Charlie Seiga was one of the most dangerous men in Britain. Men were murdered on Charlie's patch, and many times the police marked him out as a killer. The killings were swift, brutal and brilliantly organized. The victims – liberty takers and sadists – were all hard bastards who dealt in the most vicious kind of violence.

Armed to the hilt, Charlie would target the bullies who picked on weak, defenceless victims, women and the elderly. His presence was a constant challenge to the lowlife who preyed on those who could not defend themselves.

But Charlie Seiga was no angel himself. Police believed that he was the brains behind the major firms involved in bank raids, wage snatches and armed robberies involving hundreds of thousands of pounds. He lost track of the times he was arrested or questioned about various jobs, but he always had an alibi – a witness to say he wasn't guilty of the crime. He was the Houdini of the criminal world.

Charlie's story is an incredible tale of violence and crime; but it is also a story about one mans fight against the scum who break his deadly code of honour. It is the incredible autobiography of one of the most notorious figures in the history of British crime...

"After reading your brilliant book Killer; I am convinced that your story would make a compelling film...Charlie is a man who has done a lot of things in his life, always for good reason – in his eyes. The way I see it, he is no angel. Then again, he is no devil either. We'll leave it at that. One thing for sure is that he is a gentleman. Recently, I had to go to Liverpool and Charlie and his friends met me. There was a limo waiting at the station and I have to say that I was treated like a princess. Maybe it's called Liverpool hospitality. I'm not sure. Devil? Killer? But gentleman, definitely."

*– Kate Kray, crime writer and wife
of the notorious late Ronnie Kray*

"A wonderful and moving account of the trials account of the trials and struggles of one good man in a world full of unsavoury characters. This is arguably the finest 'peace, justice and the American way' genre book ever written. It moved me to tears. The author was no angel. His struggle forced him into crime. He attempted to bring down the system from within and very nearly brought it off. A great book. Buy it and read."

- W. Findlay (USA), Rated five stars on Amazon

"I believe Killer will be a major television six part drama. It is a very powerful story and I wouldn't rule out a major film theatrical production"

*- Colin McKeown, Liverpool producer whose works include
Nice Guy Eddie and Liverpool One.*

"This book brought back memories of growing up in a hard environment, one could turn to crime or make good at school. One had to fight or be walked over. Charlie tells it as it was with no holds barred. He took to crime to fulfil his dreams. I worked in the local factory as a slave to industry. Many people will relate to this book as it describes the pressure put on people trying to make a living, honestly or dishonestly. Charlie believed in certain "old fashioned values" and was willing to help the underdog. Old ladies did not go in fear of Charlie, in fact they sought his help when faced with today's drug inspired yobs. This book will be read by many all over the world who will recognise similar people in their own back yard."

- BF, Liverpool, Five star ratings.

"My parents are in their sixties and enjoyed this book as much as I did, me being in my early twenties. The book itself would be a delight to read without the dramatic impact of violence as it covers great generations of the last century. In my opinion this book stands out from the categories it is placed in and deserves a better title than 'Killer' as this limits the book far too much. Read it and you will agree."

- S.Smart, Liverpool John Moores University

"This true tale has shed a different light on the old school gangsters. Liverpool through the heart of a gentleman that decided the life of crime might be for him. Living by a code of honour that has disappeared in the villains of today. Confronted by bullies of the weak, Charlie took it upon himself to stand up and help, unlike society today. This book was written while Charlie awaits the trial for the murder of a local career criminal (taxer of weaker criminals). From the first temptation through the roller-coaster of emotions that has that can't put it down feeling. This taught my 3 teenage sons (who all read this within 24hrs, first time!) that the true to life is different from the Hollywood videos and is off putting to lead a life of crime. Words struggle to describe how gripping the book is. A real eye-opener to the underworld that has hilarious scams, illegal jobs that go right and wrong. All to earn a buck! This autobiography outrates the various fact & fiction 'best sellers' I have ever read in my life. If all 5 star reading was this good I better get a bigger bookcase! As if!"

- James Bett, Scotland

"Master criminal, scouser Charlie Seiga leads us on a rollicking rumbustuous ride through his life of crime and his dealings with blaggers, ponces, narks and the like. Throughout his career as a villain, Charlie is seen to retain the values of integrity, candour and humour, whichever difficult situation he finds himself in. His dry wit and straight talking style transfers itself beautifully to the page, making a common-or-garden novel about thieving and murder rise above anything else currently on the shelves. A unique insight into a life lived on the 'other side of the tracks'. Stop whatever you are doing. Go out. Buy it."

- Trinnie Murgatroyd, Barrow-In-Furness

The Hyenas

The Hyenas, the third and final chapter of Charlie's Autobiography, takes you up to the present day.

My name is Charlie Seiga. Armed robberies, safe-breaking, hijacking and other serious crimes were once a way of life for me. I've been charged with GBH several times, and have been in the dock for contract killings and attempted murder. In short, I was no angel – and neither were my firm.

There has always been a distinction between villains. We never beat up old men or defenceless women. Of course, there have been times when we did hurt people, and hurt them bad, but they all deserved it: women beaters, muggers, and low-life scum. I've been fighting this type throughout my life.

The old-style villain has long gone. Now the streets are full of marauding criminals with no morals, dignity or loyalty.

These are the people who got to me. Scumbags. People who would sell children to paedophiles if they thought they could make money out of it. They are called Hyenas.

They venture out at night like a gang of scavengers to carry out their so-called work. Then they return to their dens of iniquity, knowing full well that they will be hard to find if you want to hunt them down. This new breed of low-life believe they can't be hit back.

But they can. I know, because they made their biggest mistake in not killing me. I always get my revenge in the end, no matter what I have to do or how long it takes. It doesn't matter.

This is the amazing, shocking, violent and true story of my fate at the hands of the marauding low-life scum, the Hyenas.

"I think you have a wonderful story to tell and that this autobiography will sell really strongly...It's a great story, exciting and well written."

- John Blake, John Blake Publishing Limited

"I think that this book is better than killer as it's much more relevant to today's society. It flows well and the characterization is really excellent. Hugely entertaining, but also quite shocking. Brutal but honest!...I am in Belmarsh Prison in May and I am using your book in the class, to give them an example of how to go about an autobiography."

– Martina Cole, author of multiple multinational crime fictions.

"A mesmerizing book that takes you beyond Killer. This final instalment brings you right up to the present day, with Charlie Seiga's harrowing and brutal true tale. It truly is a 'can't put down' book."

- A.Maxwell, writer and book critic.

"This is the shocking story behind Charlie Seigas fate at the hands of the hyenas. The story takes you on an unmissable roller coaster of a ride from events which happened only a brief time ago. I couldn't put the book down and read from start to finish non stop, the chapters which describe the kidnapping and the following torture was like something out of a Hollywood movie, only this was for real! Having read Charlie's last book "Killer", couldn't wait for this book to be released, but was well worth it. Would definitely recommend to buy this book, UNMISSABLE!"

- Neil Honey, St.Helens, Merseyside
Amazon 5 star award

******

Charlie Seiga was born into a large family in Huyton, Merseyside in 1940. His life of crime began as a child and he became known as one of the toughest gang leaders, as well as a villain who always lived by a strict code of honour. Police believed that he was behind hundreds of bank robberies and wage snatches but remained unable to convict him.

He retired from a life of crime some years ago and still lives in Liverpool.

******